Tales from the Packers Sideline

A Collection of the Greatest Stories Ever Told

Chuck Carlson

Sports Publishing L.L.C.
www.sportspublishingllc.com

Director of production: Susan M. Moyer
Project manager: Jim Henehan
Dust jacket design: Christine Mohrbacher
Developmental editor: Kipp Wilfong
Copy editor: Cindy McNew

ISBN: 1-58261-614-0

Printed in the United States of America

Sports Publishing L.L.C.
www.sportspublishingllc.com

Contents

Acknowledgments

To do a book like this, and hopefully do it correctly, you need a lot of help. And I had plenty.

I'd like to acknowledge the folks at Sports Publishing, Mark Zulauf and Kipp Wilfong, who steered me through the project as well my old friend Bob Snodgrass, who thought of me, and enough of me, when the idea for this book was born. Many thanks also to the always helpful Green Bay Packers organization, including team president Bob Harlan, executive director of public relations Lee Remmel and Jeff Blumb, director of public relations.

I'd also like to thank everyone who offered anecdotes and stories and tales that were great to hear but that, well, couldn't be used for one reason or another. High on that list are former general manager Ron Wolf, Packers linebacker Brian Noble, and Larry McCarren, among others, as well as Mark Daniels of WGEE-AM in Green Bay, Jim Caston at WHBY-AM in Appleton and Tom Mulhern of the *Madison State Journal*. There are many, many others and I think you know who you are.

I'd also like to thank my bosses at the Oshkosh Northwestern—publisher Kevin Doyle, executive editor Stew Rieckman and sports editor Dan Kohn—for giving me the opportunity and time to write this book.

And finally thank you to Packers players and coaches, past and present, who provided me with more information that I sometimes knew what to do with.

Introduction

The story of the Green Bay Packers, and it has been chronicled more times than many people can count, is as much fiction as fact.

Indeed, who can believe a city of 90,000 souls tucked up in wintry climes of Northeastern Wisconsin could be the home of an NFL franchise? Who could believe that same franchise could survive and, ultimately, thrive over a history that spans 85 years? And who could believe that same franchise could win 12 world titles, including three Super Bowls, while franchises in much larger and in supposedly more progressive cities have yet to win one?

And who could believe that same franchise could produce players like this: Don Hutson, Tony Canadeo, Johnny "Blood" McNally, Dave Robinson, Paul Hornung, Ray Nitschke, Bart Starr, Jerry Kramer, James Lofton, Sterling Sharpe, Brett Favre and so many others while being coached by the likes of Curly Lambeau, Vince Lombardi and Mike Holmgren?

It is not a story to be believed, but it happened and it continues to happen.

The Packers are as much a part of the NFL, and of Americana, as anything you could name. The classic white block "G" on the side of the yellow helmets is as recognizable a symbol as the golden arches or the New York Yankees pinstripes.

Today, the Packers remain one of the most popular sports franchises in the nation. There are fan clubs spread not only throughout the country, but around the world. A fan club in Poland, in fact, boasts more than 500 members. There are self-titled "Packers" bars located in California, Florida, Colorado and Texas. A little bar in the beach community of Dewey Beach, Delaware is called "The Frozen Tundra."

So the Packers reach everywhere, and the effect is huge. And when the Packers win, more than just fans in Wisconsin celebrate the occasion.

Many is the day, in fact, even in the bleakest days of winter, when the season is over and a savage wind blows through the Lambeau Field parking lot, that people will still drive up, pose in front of the stadium, snap a photo and drive away.

"I love it when they do that," team president Bob Harlan said. "That tells me a lot."

Harlan often watches from his office high atop the refurbished stadium as limousines pull up and a wedding party—complete with a bride all in white and groom in a tux—scramble out, have a picture taken and clambered back in.

On a recent snowy day, three people decked out in Oakland Raiders regalia stopped and had a picture taken.

"It's Lambeau Field," one person said. "We had to do it."

This is what the Green Bay Packers, and everything surrounding them, means to a lot of people, even if no one can really explain it.

"It's the David vs. Goliath mentality," longtime Packers public relations director Lee Remmel said.

It's ironic that nearly 10 years ago, a young whipper-snapper of a quarterback named Brett Favre made a prophetic statement as the Packers were beginning their rise back to prominence. It was back in the days when the Dallas Cowboys were the kings of the NFL and playing to the hilt their role as "America's Team."

"When the Cowboys won the Super Bowl, Dallas went crazy," he said at the time. "When the Packers win the Super Bowl again, all America will go crazy."

He was right, because four years later, the Packers did indeed win another Super Bowl, and the celebration stretched from one end of the country to the other.

That's because the Packers represent everything that was simple and good about the NFL. It's a blue-collar team cheered on by fans who work in foundries and factories and paper mills. And a game at Lambeau Field, even though its $295 million facelift has changed much of how the place looks, is still an experience like no other. To cheer for the Packers is to cheer for the perpetual underdog.

And the stories ... Oh, the stories. They have come down the line from everyone and everywhere. You can't find anyone in Wisconsin who doesn't know Packers stories, real or imagined. That's because for years the Packers not only played in Green Bay, many lived here and opened businesses within a 30-mile radius of Green Bay called the Fox Valley.

Many were the nights when fans would report interesting goings-on at an Appleton restaurant/bar called The Left Guard, an establishment run by former Packer Jerry Kramer.

The Packers were a part of the community. Vince Lombardi could be seen walking to the dry cleaners and Mike Holmgren would be stopped in a grocery store and told to beat the Bears. It is the state's team, and the fans protect that with a jealous pride.

So there are always stories, plenty of stories. From the days of Curly Lambeau and the infancy of the NFL all the way until today under coach/general manager Mike Sherman as the Packers have regained their spot among the NFL's elite.

All the stories are good; some are probably even true. But perhaps the best story of all is about the Green Bay

Brett Favre has taken his place among the best and most popular players the Green Bay Packers organization has ever known. And he almost didn't make it there after failing his first physical with the team. *Photo courtesy of Vernon J. Biever*

Packers franchise itself. In today's world, it should not exist. It is too small, too provincial, too Midwest, too everything and too not enough. But here it sits and here it stays, a study in contradictions.

And a great story, too.

Tales

It's Called Green Bay

It remains one of Reggie White's favorite stories, and it can serve as a testament to nearly every football player who ended up coming to Green Bay and making it their home away from home.

"When I played in Philadelphia, the one thing the coaches told us was, 'If you screw up, we're going to trade you to Green Bay,'" White said. "That was the worst thing we could think of."

And, at the time, Green Bay was indeed an NFL version of a Soviet gulag, where players would go when they had nowhere else to go. Bad weather, bad teams, bad image, bad everything, and whoever did end up there knew that, in many respects, Green Bay was their last chance.

"I lived here year-round, so I was making other teams pay," joked longtime linebacker Brian Noble, a Southern California native who did indeed make Wisconsin home. "I was stuck in Green Bay, and I was going to make somebody pay for it on the field."

Ron Wolf knew all about it, too.

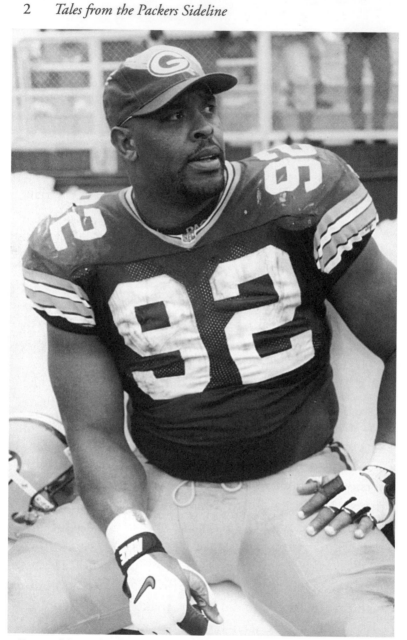

Everything changed for the Packers when Reggie White shocked the NFL by signing as a free agent with the Packers in 1993. *Photo courtesy of Vernon J. Biever*

"You can't imagine the number of people who told me I was making a career mistake going to Green Bay," Wolf said. "It was a horror show. It was a deathbed for anyone who wanted to go there."

But team president Bob Harlan had a vision for the franchise in the early 1990s, and Wolf was his man to put that vision in focus. "I talked to [then New York Giants general manager] George Young and he told me at the time that I'd never get Ron Wolf out of New York," Harlan said. "But I knew it was worth a try."

Indeed, the two men had talked to each other a couple of years earlier when Wolf was a candidate for player personnel director, a job that ultimately went to Tom Braatz after Wolf withdrew his name.

Even then Harlan was impressed. But Wolf wasn't ready for the Packers and, frankly, the Packers weren't ready for Wolf.

"I never had any impression of the Packers before I came there," Wolf said.

"I was an old AFL and then an AFC guy. That's the league I knew. Aside from the aura of Vince Lombardi, I didn't know anything about it."

But when Harlan offered Wolf the kind of unilateral power no Packer general manager had known since Lombardi, he jumped at the opportunity.

"I was so tired of losing," Harlan said.

For a job so all-encompassing, the negotiations were quick. Harlan told Wolf what his powers would be, and Wolf always swore he'd keep Harlan informed of his decisions.

"And we never had a cross word," Harlan said.

That was November, 1991. In the ensuing weeks, Wolf fired head coach Lindy Infante, hired Mike Holmgren, traded for Brett Favre, revamped the scouting system, spent millions on new training facilities and then watched as everything he wished for fell into place.

In fact, on a brutal, brittle January afternoon in 1997, Wolf's eyes flamed as he watched his team collect the NFC championship trophy at Lambeau Field.

"That moment right there encompasses all of my 40 years in football," Wolf said.

"There's never been a moment like that for me."

What's In a Color?

Perhaps nothing is more identifiable with the Green Bay Packers than the distinctive green and gold colors that became a staple in the 1950s. The block "G," the green jerseys, the gold helmets, they all signified something very special, very unusual, very Green Bay.

But when Ron Wolf took over as general manager in 1991, he was ready to change everything regarding the franchise—and that meant from the front office to the practice facilities to how people went about their daily duties. It also meant tinkering with, or at least thinking about tinkering with, the most established part of the Packers aura—the team colors.

"I went before the executive committee and asked them, 'Why not change the colors?'" Wolf said, clearly not understanding that if he changed the Packers colors, he might as well come out against Santa Claus while he was at it.

"It wasn't even really a gold color," Wolf said. "It was a kind of yellow. I just didn't like it."

Wolf commissioned some design changes—some that were subtle and some that weren't. He looked at replacing the mustardy yellow color with more of a gold (similar to what the St. Louis Rams use today) that would be more in keeping with the Packers' history of green and gold.

But as with most things Packers, word leaked out to the public that the new guy in town was going to change the team colors into God knows what. Team president Bob Harlan was deluged with phone calls from irate fans who couldn't understand why the Packers would even think of altering the colors.

And in the end, Wolf agreed, though not because of any major fan backlash.

"We had some drawings made and it just looked awful," Wolf said. "You could look at all the drawings and pictures you want, but until you see it, you don't know. And when I saw it I hated it. So we decided to just stay where we are."

It may have been one of the best decisions, or non-decisions, he ever made.

The Quarterback

Packers fans are weaned on the story of just how Brett Favre made it to Green Bay and the confluence of luck and instinct that made it work.

For Ron Wolf, trading for Brett Favre was the centerpiece of the rebuilding project of the Green Bay Packers and, unknown to this day, he almost never made it here.

Given the kind of power unknown to a Packers general
manager since the days of Vince Lombardi, Ron Wolf
turned the Packers from an NFL doormat into a perennial
powerhouse. *Photo courtesy of Vernon J. Biever*

Wolf had been interested in Favre from his junior year at Southern Mississippi when he was a reckless and fearless gunslinger. But Favre had been injured his senior year at Southern Miss and his stock had fallen in the eyes of many NFL scouts—except Wolf.

As player personnel director with the Jets, Wolf desperately wanted to draft Favre, but Favre slipped away and was drafted by the Atlanta Falcons instead, where he wallowed on the bench and in the doghouse of then coach Jerry Glanville.

Almost immediately after being hired by the Packers, Wolf went to Atlanta, where the Packers had a game that Sunday, to watch Favre throw in pregame warmups. But Wolf soon learned that Favre wouldn't be throwing much before the game. He hustled down from the press box, was caught up in traffic and interviews and never saw his prized possession throw. Still, Wolf knew all he needed to know, and the deal—a straight-up No. 1 pick to the Falcons for Favre—was consummated.

So confident was Wolf that he never drew up language in the contract about Favre's abilty to pass a Packers team physical to complete the deal.

And Favre didn't pass his physical. Various ailments from a sore knee to a bum shoulder put the deal in jeopardy until Wolf took matters in his own hands.

"I sent him back over for another physical, and I said [to the doctors], 'He's going to pass,'" Wolf said. "And he did. I mean, I pinned my career on that guy."

Mike Sherman, Revealed

He is a stoic, unknowable man who seems to hide his emotions so deep inside that no one can find them. But Mike Sherman, the Packers coach and general manager, has his moments.

There was the time, on a drive through Door County, Wis., where his family owns a summer home, when he saw a lonely bar sitting out in an empty field. Curious as to why the bar was there by itself, he stopped one lazy summer afternoon to visit with the patrons, drink some beer and find out about the place.

"An older woman is the bartender and she recognizes him, and he sits there talking to her and the people in that bar," president Bob Harlan said. "And I thought, 'How many Packers head coaches would do that?' There's a warmth there, there's a down-to-earth quality. He's what you draw up if you wanted a head coach of the Green Bay Packers. He loves the tradition."

Indeed, during the reconstruction of Lambeau Field, Sherman learned that the door frame from the sainted Vince Lombardi's office was embedded in a wall in the old administration building. He had maintenance people dig through the wall, find the door frame and make it part of the door frame of his new office.

"I want some of Coach Lombardi to rub off on me," he said simply.

He also took three slabs of concrete from the old tunnel leading out to Lambeau Field and had it moved into the new tunnel surrounded by bricks. "He has a wonderful feel for the tradition," Harlan said.

Mike Sherman, an obscure tight ends coach for a year under Mike Holmgren, returned to Green Bay in 2000 to take over as head coach and, amazingly, a year later also general manager. *Photo courtesy of Vernon J. Biever*

The Man In Charge

Bob Harlan still answers his own phone. No matter if it's the NFL commissioner or just a fan from down the street, he takes all the calls—and the heat. He joined the organization on June 1, 1971, a 34-year-old kid who did everything from negotiating contracts to running the marketing department. Since then, Harlan has overseen some of the most volcanic changes in club history. "Before I was hired [as team president in 1989], the only real question the executive board had for me was could I make the tough decisions," Harlan said with a laugh. "I think I've shown I can do that."

It began with the hiring of Ron Wolf as general manager in 1991 and supplying him with the kind of power not given to a Packers GM since Vince Lombardi. It followed with his decision in 1995 to move out of Milwaukee and decrepit County Stadium, where they had played three home games and a preseason game every year for more than 50 years.

It was a decision that enraged Milwaukee season ticket holders, many of whom had been on board since the beginning when the Packers needed Milwaukee to bail the franchise out of a financial debacle. And now, in their view, Harlan was turning his back on the biggest city in the state.

But Harlan also knew that by leaving Milwaukee, the Packers would gain $2 million per game, crucial for a franchise like Green Bay. He also appeased the Milwaukee fan base by offering a new season ticket package that would give County Stadium season ticket holders three games a year.

But his biggest project was marshalling through a $295 million renovation project on Lambeau Field that Harlan was convinced was needed to keep the team competitive.

It was a bruising battle that saw Harlan go to every corner of the state drumming up support and convincing fans of its necessity. The problem was a 1/2 of 1 percent sales tax on Brown County residents to help pay for the project.

Harlan took his share of blows in the battle, but in the end, a Brown County referendum passed, and the project is slated for completion this summer.

"I'd do it all again, too," Harlan said.

Mount Holmgren

For all of his silky ease and game show host personality, a fearsome temper burned just below the surface of coach Mike Holmgren.

Players would routinely talk of his thunderous tirades at halftime of games the Packers were sleepwalking through. In practice, he would drop enough F-bombs to make Marine drill sergeants blush. And he would hold grudges. Oh my, would he hold grudges. He would routinely bench a player for fumbling, the one trait he could not abide and, indeed, even traded one promising running back, Ahman Green, when he was in Seattle because of his penchant for putting the ball on the ground. Green ended up in Green Bay and is now a Pro Bowler.

But that's Holmgren.

There are dozens of memorable examples of his temper getting the better of him, but here are just a few.

In 1998, as the Packers were struggling at home against the woeful Eagles and rumors were already flying about Holmgren's desire to leave Green Bay, a fan squawked at Holmgren as he headed to the locker room for halftime.

"Keep your head in the game," the fan screamed. "You're still coaching here, you know."

Holmgren sought out the fan, pointed his finger at him and began one of his famous blue-streaked tirades before security moved him into the tunnel.

It was an unfortunate and embarrassing incident that Holmgren apologized for but which was another sign that his days in Green Bay were numbered.

Two incidents arose in the Metrodome in Minneapolis, where the Packers have never played well.

In 1997, the Packers were actually on their way to a huge win over the Minnesota Vikings when, late in the game, backup wide receiver Bill Schroeder was called for an unnecessary roughness penalty on a kickoff that gave the Vikings great field position.

Holmgren was so angry with Schroeder that he grabbed him by the shoulder pads and screamed at him in a scene played out for a TV crowd on Monday night.

Holmgren took his share of abuse from fans for his treatment of Schroeder, who, frankly, deserved the rebuke for the stupid penalty. And this time, Holmgren didn't apologize.

Two years earlier, in one of the more infamous moments in Packers history, the Packers were again on their way to a victory. Brett Favre had already been knocked out of the game with an ankle injury and backup Ty Detmer went down with a thumb injury. That left the No. 3 quarterback, T. J. Rubley, to run the show. And he did a creditable enough job, driving the Packers into

**He was the hottest NFL coaching prospect in 1992, and
when Mike Holmgren rejected offers from two other teams
to join the Packers, it marked a new era for the franchise.**
Photo courtesy of Vernon J. Biever

Vikings territory late in the game to set up what should have been a game-winning field goal.

Then it got interesting. Rubley decided to audible out of a play Holmgren called (never a good idea in the best of circumstances), changing a running play to a pass. The throw was intercepted, the Vikings held on and the Packers absorbed a tough defeat.

So angry was Holmgren afterward that on the walk up the tunnel to the locker room, he smashed his fist against a light fixture, shattering the light and, rumor has it, causing a hairline fracture in his hand. No one ever saw a cast on Holmgren's hand, but the story has become part of Packers legend.

Rubley, by the way, was released two weeks later.

Rhodes to Nowhere

It wasn't often that Ron Wolf admitted he was wrong, but with his hiring of Ray Rhodes to replace Mike Holmgren as head coach, he admitted it was a blunder.

"It just didn't work out," Wolf said. "I thought I knew who I was hiring and I was wrong. I did not do justice to the Green Bay Packers."

Wolf was convinced that the Packers needed a strong presence to replace Holmgren, and he was certain Rhodes, who was coming off a tough season in Philadelphia, was the guy. Tough, no-nonsense and blunt, Rhodes would be the perfect match for a Packers team Wolf was still convinced was championship material.

But it didn't take long for Wolf to realize he was wrong. Blunders on the field, including an inexcusable decision

Ray Rhodes replaced Mike Holmgren in 1999, and it became evident early that it wasn't going to work out. He was fired after one season. *Photo courtesy of Vernon J. Biever*

not to call timeouts late in a loss to Carolina, were part of the problem. Another was what he observed in practice.

"The team was dead," Wolf said. "For whatever reason, the players just didn't respond to Ray. The team had no life and it had to change."

Wolf wrestled with the decision about what to do, to the point that he was in constant contact with Harlan, who was back in Iowa tending to his ill mother. Harlan even brought a cell phone with him so that Wolf could contact him. One night the phone rang and Wolf was on the other end.

"Just wanted to make sure the number works," Wolf said.

But immediately after the season finale, a win over Arizona, Wolf called Harlan and told him of his decision.

"I told Ron to do whatever he saw fit," Harlan said.

That night, Wolf informed Rhodes he was being fired, even though the Packers finished 8-8 and barely missed the playoffs.

"I'd have made the same decision even if we'd made the playoffs," Wolf said. "It couldn't continue like this. It was horrible. Those things are not pleasant, but somebody had to do it."

Wolf had interviewed no one else before hiring Rhodes, and he wasn't going to make that same mistake with this decision.

He interviewed half a dozen high-profile coaches and coordinators before settling on the person no one expected, Mike Sherman.

Mike Who?

The decision to hire the unknown Sherman caught everyone by surprise, even Ron Wolf, who was blown away by the mild-mannered New Englander and his staggering sense of organization.

"He had his practice schedule mapped out for the entire year," Wolf said. "It was incredible."

Bob Harlan, who gave Wolf carte blanche to hire whomever he saw fit, remembers the story.

"I never said more than hello to Mike when he was here before [as tight ends coach under Holmgren]," Harlan said.

"It was a Saturday morning, and I was downstairs when Ron and Mike walked by [during the interview]. We shook hands and I said hello and welcome and I didn't see them the rest of the day.

"About 4 o'clock that afternoon my phone rings at home and it's Ron. And Ron never calls me at home. He said, 'If I had any guts at all I'd hire Mike Sherman right now.' And I said, 'Go ahead.'"

This was at the same time that Marty Schottenheimer, the former Cleveland Browns and Kansas City Chiefs coach, was believed to be the front-runner. But Wolf was so impressed with Sherman and his vision of the future that, suddenly, all bets were off.

Wolf decided to think overnight about whether to hire Sherman or not, and he came back to Harlan the next morning.

That next morning, Harlan was meeting with several other executives about the substantial financial demands of Schottenheimer when Wolf knocked on the door.

"Tell you what, if I had any guts I'd hire Sherman right now," Wolf said.

Harlan said, "Why not?"

Less than five minutes later, Wolf was back and said, "It's done."

The rest, as they say, is history.

Learning the Story

Not everyone is familiar with the Green Bay Packers story, and one day president Bob Harlan ran into a new player, Los Angeles native and San Diego State University graduate Kabeer Gbaja-Biamila, a defensive end whom Harlan couldn't wait to indoctrinate.

"Right after we drafted Kabeer we had a mini-camp and I was sitting in my office one afternoon," Harlan said.

"I looked up and Kabeer is standing in the doorway. He and I had never even seen each other before. He said 'I'm Kabeer', and I said, 'I'm Bob, what can I do for you?'"

The player who would come to be known as "KGB" asked simply, "What goes on up here?" and Harlan was only too glad to show him.

Harlan took him on a tour, including the board room, and told him about the executive committee and the fact that there is no single owner, that the team sold stock, and that if at any time the team had to fold, the proceeds would go to the Green Bay Packers Foundation, a charitable organization, and the franchise would simply cease to function.

"He was listening, but he wasn't asking a lot of questions," Harlan said.

Harlan then showed him the accounting department and public relations and explained just how important the Packers are to the community, not only as a football team, but as a force in society.

"We were probably together 15 or 20 minutes and he asks, 'Bob, what do you do here?'" Harlan said.

Harlan laughed and replied, "Well, when I'm not giving tours, I'm the president."

The gregarious Gbaja-Biamila roared with laughter and said, "I guess I shouldn't be calling you Bob."

Harlan said simply, "Everybody calls me Bob."

To this day, Gbaja-Biamila still visits Harlan in his office and threatens, one day, to take it over for himself.

The Tradition

Ron Wolf remembers walking through a department store in Green Bay soon after he was hired as general manager and recalling how little Packers paraphernalia he saw.

"There was a lot of University of Wisconsin stuff but very little Packers," he said. "I thought that was odd."

But that soon changed. As the Packers began to win, the fire began to burn again in Packers fans, who had always continued to show up for games through two decades of mediocrity but had learned not to expect much.

Five years after Wolf arrived, the Packers were second among NFL teams in merchandise sold, trailing only the Dallas Cowboys. Today they remain one of the NFL's top sellers as well as one of the best among all sports teams.

"This is really America's team," Wolf has said more than once.

Moreover, despite removing several thousand names from the season ticket waiting list with the expansion of Lambeau Field, more than 50,000 names still remain on the list. Wolf may not have understood when he first came to Green Bay what the franchise meant, but he certainly understood by the time he left.

"It's a marvelous tradition," he said. "The league fathers have to keep Green Bay. It's the pro football Mecca. It's where it started, and the Green Bay Packers have to be part of it because of the tradition. And if you don't have the tradition, you don't have anything."

The Frozen What?

You can still hear the unforgettable voice of NFL Films narrator John Facenda as you look out on Lambeau Field.

And you hear that phrase: "The frozen tundra."

No one really knows where it came from or who started it, but it is almost impossible now, especially when they play in winter (which sometimes starts in October, but that's another story), to watch a Packers game without the field being referred to as the frozen tundra.

Of course, what it lacks in accuracy it more than makes up for in stunning imagery.

Name someone other than a hockey player who wants to play on anything frozen. More to the point, find anyone who wants to play on something that's called tundra.

It evokes stark images of treeless plains and flying snow and the odd woolly mammoth tromping by. And maybe that's one of the reasons the Packers have always been so good in cold weather.

From 1992, when then coach Mike Holmgren made it a top priority for his teams to be next to unbeatable at home, to today, the Packers know that when the mercury falls, their chances of losing also fall.

Just in playoff games, with the temperature 34 degrees or lower, the Packers are 11-1 at Lambeau Field. From 1992-2002, the Packers have lost just four regular-season games at Lambeau in the months of November, December and January.

"We just know we can't lose here," longtime safety LeRoy Butler said.

It has reached a point where opponents have begun to believe it, too. Whether it's the temperature or the crowd or the setting, other teams know that to beat the Packers at Lambeau Field requires a Herculean effort that most team aren't capable of providing.

The mystique did end in the 2002 season, however, when the Packers lost in the opening round of the playoffs to the Atlanta Falcons amidst snow flurries and 25-degree temperatures.

Ironically, the Falcons also beat the Packers at Lambeau Field in November, 2001 and nearly beat them in the home opener in 2002 before Green Bay prevailed in overtime. So whatever it is the Falcons have discovered, the rest of the NFL would like a bottle.

That playoff loss also brought a sour end to a season that saw the Packers go unbeaten at home in the regular season—the only team in the NFL to accomplish that.

But back to the frozen tundra.

Lake Superior State University in Michigan recently compiled a "List of Words Banished from the Queen's English for Mis-Use, Over-Use and General Uselessness" and, that's right, "frozen tundra" was there.

The complaint? Tundra is already frozen land, so to call it frozen tundra is to be redundant.

When Packers fans became aware of the assault on their prized phrase, they reacted as you'd expect Packers fans to react—they ignored it.

Even Remmel got into the scrum.

"Redundant or not, I think it's a phrase that's here to stay," he said.

For too many fans, there is no Lambeau Field without the frozen tundra preceding it. And the Packers will certainly continue to use it to their advantage every season when the weather cools and the snow flies and teams know they will have to play three hours in someplace they really don't want to be.

Leaping in Lambeau

It's another Packers tradition steeped in mystery and bathed in mythology.

The Lambeau leap, now as much a part of Packers games as cold hot dogs and hot beer, came out of nowhere, really, and was more of a lark than anything. Indeed the inventor, safety LeRoy Butler, had no idea what he was doing that icy December day when he decided that a touchdown celebration should include the fans in a deep and intimate way. If he'd known how it would catch on, and many teams throughout the league have their own version of it now, he might have sought a patent and really made some money off of it.

Consider the scene: It was a late-season, meaningless game against the Los Angeles Raiders on one of those mind-numbingly cold days in Green Bay.

"It was like 42 degrees below zero and the field was frozen," Butler said. "Everything was frozen."

On a Raiders screen pass, Butler hit the receiver and the ball came loose. Defensive end Reggie White scooped it up and began lumbering toward the end zone. Realizing he wasn't going to make it before a Raider lineman reached him, White pitched the ball back to the trailing Butler, who took it down the left sideline for the touchdown that sealed the win.

"As I was running, the crowd was going crazy," Butler recalled. "They were reaching down and patting the side of the stadium. It was all spontaneous."

Butler reached the end zone and kept running, leaping into the north bleachers, where giddy Packers fans awaited, pummeling and pounding him in celebration.

A tradition was born.

The craze really took off in 1995 when wide receiver Robert Brooks would vault into the crowd after scoring. Soon, other teammates who scored decided to leap.

By the Packers' Super Bowl-winning season of 1996, nearly every Packer who scored a touchdown leaped into the stands to be drowned by a green and gold sea of delirious fans. It even became more refined as two Packers at once would jump or sometimes there would be a delayed jump.

Even today, the tradition remains strong, though admittedly not as many Packers perform the Lambeau Leap as they once did. Halfback Ahman Green won't do it, nor will tight end Bubba Franks, but they weren't even around when the tradition began.

Quarterback Brett Favre never has and never will leap, though teammates claim that he couldn't jump that high, anyway.

But it remains a goal for many young Packers who score. Wide receiver Donald Driver scored a preseason touchdown as a rookie and sprinted to the stands, where he immediately slipped and fell on his rear end. But he completed it nonetheless.

As for the coaching staff's view of the leap, it remains the same as it always was: It's fine, just as long as the fans throw the player back.

The Lion Kings

It seemed like a good idea at the time, or at least it did to a couple of young Packers running backs— Travis Jervey and LeShon Johnson by name.

It was 1995 and both were battling for backup roles in the Packers' backfield. But just because they were rivals for the same position didn't mean they weren't good friends. In fact, they were roommates during the season and grew to enjoy the same things.

For instance, both were cited that season by the state's Department of Natural Resources for illegal deer snares in back of their houses in the Wisconsin woods.

But midway through the season, Johnson, a second-year back, and Jervey, with a surfer-dude haircut and attitude to match, decided on an even stranger scheme.

Convinced they needed something to spice up their existence beyond the football field, the two players ordered a lion from a wildlife distributor in Texas.

The two paid $1,000 for the carnivore that, according to Jervey, wasn't dangerous because he'd been declawed and had his canine teeth removed. Still, coach Mike

Holmgren would have none of it and told the two to cancel the order.

After getting wind of the transaction, the rest of the Packers had their fun with it. At practice that week, both players, instead of having their names on the back of their practice jerseys as usual, had the name "Lion King" stitched on the back.

But Jervey was undaunted and was considering ordering a tiger instead. Jervey left the Packers four years later in free agency, and Johnson was cut the following season.

Aside from his taste in pets, Jervey was also known for his rather eclectic choice of where to live. Though a graduate of the rock-ribbed Citadel, where he is still the school's all-time leading rusher, Jervey always loved the ocean and surfing.

In fact, when he was named to the Pro Bowl as a special teams player in 1997, Jervey couldn't wait to go to Hawaii (where the game is held every year) and hit the surf, even though he'd had a no-surfing clause inserted in his contract.

It's also why he chose an unusual spot to build a new home—Costa Rica.

Jervey went to the Central American country for vacation a year earlier and fell in love with the varied climate and topography.

"You can go from the beach to the mountains in an hour," he said.

He was also pleased with the lack of political upheaval normally associated with Central America.

"It's really great," he said. "It's neutral. It's sort of like the Switzerland of Central America."

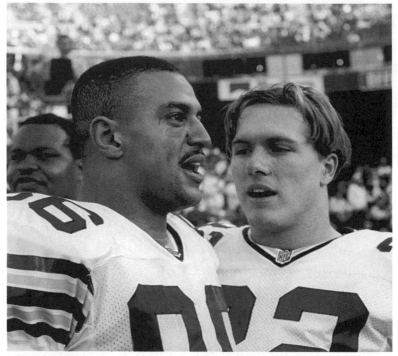

Travis Jervey, seen here on the right with wide receiver Antonio Freeman, was a special teams demon and an eclectic character, to say the least. *Photo courtesy of Vernon J. Biever*

The Christmas Miracle

When Reggie White joined the Green Bay Packers, everything changed. The old set of rules no longer applied. When Reggie White ended what was then the NFL's most intense free agency battle by shocking the world and signing with Green Bay, suddenly the playing field was even for everyone.

"I thought we'd have a chance to sign him, but I really wasn't sure," former general manager Ron Wolf said. "I mean, everyone wanted him."

Maybe not everyone, but the NFL's big hitters at the time—the San Francisco 49ers and Washington Redskins, among others—certainly did.

But prior to the 1993 season, White, claiming he'd heard a voice from God, signed with the Packers because "God told me to." Cynics believed differently and believed it wasn't necessarily a higher power, but the $17 million the Packers were going to pay him over the life of the contract that made the difference.

Whatever it was, the Packers suddenly went from one of the NFL's loneliest outposts to a serious, viable title contender.

White was everything he was advertised to be. He led the team in sacks in two of his first three seasons and was on his way to another great season in 1995 when disaster struck in a December 3 game against the Cincinnati Bengals.

As White was bearing down on Bengals quarterback Neil O'Donnell for a sack, White suddenly collapsed to the ground, holding his left leg in agony.

The diagnosis wasn't good: It was a torn hamstring, the kind of injury that bedeviled the Packers for several years and ended the careers of two players, center James Campen and promising rookie center Mark D'Onofrio.

And it didn't appear much better for White, whose age and the location of the injury worked against him. At a minimum, team doctors believed White was done for the rest of the season, and if the injury didn't heal properly, he could be done for good.

The Packers got a distasteful look at the future without Reggie when they went to Tampa and lost to the awful Buccaneers. But even then White, who made the trip with the team, was noticing something was changing. The leg, which had been in agony all week, was starting to feel better.

Then, during the week prior to the Packers trip to New Orleans to face the Saints, White was lying on the training room table getting more of the non-stop treatment. During the treatment he fell asleep, and when he awoke, the leg no longer hurt. He got up and walked around, and the limp was gone. The torn hamstring, which should have ended his season and might have ended his career, had somehow healed, according to White.

That night, White went over to coach Mike Holmgren's house to tell him he was ready to play against the Saints. Holmgren was in the midst of putting up Christmas lights on his house when his star defensive end showed up with his shocking announcement. Holmgren was incredulous and unconvinced until he put White through drills in practice that week and he came through with flying colors.

"It was a miracle," White said in a press conference to the dubious media that week. "You guys may not believe it, but you should. God healed me."

And indeed Reggie White was on the field when the Packers clinched a playoff berth with a win over the Saints.

"I'll never doubt Reggie again," Holmgren said.

The Quarterback, Part II

That same season, quarterback Brett Favre also showed remarkable recuperative powers and went a long way toward sealing his place in Packers lore.

In a November 5 contest against the Minnesota Vikings in a place that would prove to be Favre's, and the Packers', personal hell, the Metrodome, Favre severely sprained his left ankle when his right tackle, Aaron Taylor, fell on him. Favre missed the rest of that game, which the Packers lost, and after the game, he was on crutches, the left ankle dangling helplessly in an air cast.

Already understanding even then that the Packers' fortunes were inextricably tied to No. 4, the questions began almost immediately about whether Favre could play the following week in a key matchup against their ancient rival, the Chicago Bears.

All week Holmgren maintained that he didn't know the status of his star quarterback, though deep down he knew only too well. He had seen the ankle and he had watched as Favre tried to walk on it, and he knew there was no way he'd be ready for the Bears. The guy couldn't even move without help, and he was going to try to avoid a pass rush? Impossible.

Sensing a growing disaster, Holmgren did what he'd never done before and closed practice that week to the media. Normally, Holmgren was as accommodating as necessary with the people who covered the team, but this was different. This was bunker mentality time, and he needed time to plot and scheme and figure out what to do without his unquestioned leader.

What made the situation worse was that backup quarterback Ty Detmer was also injured in the Vikings' game and was unavailable. That left No. 3 quarterback T. J. Rubley, whom Holmgren did not trust after his debacle the previous week when he called an audible on a late drive and was intercepted.

Desperate, Holmgren called on old-timer Bob Gagliano, who had played for Holmgren in San Francisco when he was quarterbacks coach and then offensive coordinator. Gagliano was pulled out of semi-retirement because of his maturity and his experience in running the Holmgren style of the so-called West Coast offense. And all this was done behind closed doors.

By Saturday, Favre, who had received 24-hour treatment on his ankle, was at least able to move on his own, and he made the startling revelation that, just maybe, he could make a go of it against the Bears.

And on Sunday, with an ankle taped so heavily that it was as hard as a cast, Favre limped out on the field. He took part in no pregame drills, instead watching from the side with his hands jammed in his jersey pockets. Then came game time, and Favre was where he was always meant to be—under center and ready to go.

All he did after that was respond with perhaps the greatest performance of his career and one of the gutsiest in NFL history.

"I've never seen better," Packers PR director Lee Remmel said.

Favre completed 25 of 33 passes for 336 yards with no interceptions and a personal-best and team record-tying five touchdown passes. The Packers won 35-28, and the Brett Favre legend took even deeper root.

Lost in the hoopla of that remarkable performance was the fact that the following week, Favre may have been even better. With the ankle still a major concern (eventually it required off-season surgery to repair) and cutting again into his practice time, he took the Packers to Cleveland, where two weeks earlier it had been announced that the Browns were leaving for a better deal in Baltimore.

In a gray, angry Municipal Stadium, Favre was on target with 23 of 28 passes for 210 yards. He threw for three more touchdowns and, amazingly, ran for another, limping into the end zone and spiking the ball triumphantly.

But he wasn't finished that season.

In the season finale at Lambeau Field against the rugged Pittsburgh Steelers, the Packers found themselves in a war. And Favre took the brunt of the abuse.

He was knocked senseless three different times by the Steelers' swarming defense, the worst coming as he tried to score from a yard out before being clobbered by linebacker Kevin Greene. He was hit so hard that, after being helped up to his feet, he spit up blood.

The Packers called a timeout and, in that time, Favre recovered his senses, went back in the game and threw a touchdown pass to tight end Mark Chmura. The Packers won, 24-19, and the Packers clinched the NFC Central Division title for the first time since 1972.

It was an incredible season for Favre as he threw for an NFL-best 4,413 yards and 38 touchdowns while throwing only 13 interceptions. Not surprisingly, he earned the first of his three straight NFL MVP honors.

The Sharper Image

He was the enigma in green and gold. Affable and vociferous on the practice field with his teammates, he was surly and unknowable off the field with everyone else. A breathtaking talent on the field, he was irascible and infuriating everywhere else.

Smart and funny, angry and uncooperative, Sterling Sharpe was without question one of the greatest wide receivers in Packers history and, had it not been for a neck injury that prematurely ended his career, he would have been a lock to make the Pro Football Hall of Fame.

But Sharpe not only marched to a different drummer, he demanded to be in charge of the entire band, and as a result, his departure prior to the 1995 season wasn't exactly mourned by teammates or fans.

He was the Packers' top draft pick in 1988, and he came to Green Bay with a refreshing, upfront attitude that included a commitment to always be open with the local media that covered the team.

And in his first season Sharpe was solid enough, leading the Packers with 55 receptions and averaging 14 yards a catch. But he also dropped far too many passes, a fact that was brought out by the local media, especially the hometown *Green Bay Press-Gazette*. Stung by the scrutiny, Sharpe shut down and stopped talking. It was a practice he continued for the remainder of his career, though he would conduct interviews with national media outlets.

The resulting blackout left the impression with Packers fans that he didn't care about the team or the community, which, in truth, he probably didn't. Sharpe came from the school that subscribed to doing his job the best he could. He didn't like signing autographs and he detested the trappings of notoriety, which in a fishbowl like Green Bay was nearly impossible to escape.

So the minute the season ended, Sharpe fled Green Bay for his home in South Carolina (as did nearly every other player, for that matter), though during the season he was the consummate professional.

And Sharpe quickly developed into one of the NFL's top receivers, blessed with great hands and a fearlessness in going over the middle when no other receiver would. He could take punishment and deal it out and still gain yards when necessary. He caught 90 passes his second season when the Packers went 10-6 and barely missed the playoffs before slumping back to 67 in 1990 when quarterback woes plagued the Packers all season.

By 1992, though, Mike Holmgren had taken over as head coach and Brett Favre was eventually established as the quarterback and Sharpe flourished. In his first season under Holmgren, Sharpe set what was then an NFL record with 108 receptions and scored 13 touchdowns. But instead of enjoying the moment and the spotlight, Sharpe maintained his policy of ignoring the local media.

Indeed, in the game where he set the record, a season-ending 27-7 loss to the Vikings that kept the Packers from securing a playoff bid, Sharpe was nowhere to be found after the game.

Instead of talking, even briefly, about the record, the reticent receiver remained holed up in the training room so he wouldn't have to face the cameras and tape recorders. Despite a plea from the media for even a statement, Sharpe would not relent. Teammates simply rolled their eyes and shrugged as if to say, "That's Sterling."

And that was Sterling, because, for better or worse, he was who he was and he cared not at all what people thought of him.

Favre and Sharpe always had a prickly relationship at best, because the two approached the game so differently. Favre was exuberant and childlike, someone for whom football was everything. Sharpe viewed it as a job to be done and little more.

But as cold and distant as he could be with so many people, including the guys he played with, he was always there when it mattered. In his final season, when a chronic and agonizing toe injury kept him from running full speed, much less practicing, he was there on Sundays and ended up catching a team-best 94 passes with a staggering 18 touchdowns.

Yet it was also that season when Sharpe might well have lost the respect of the other Packers when, a day before the season opener against the Vikings, Sharpe threatened not to play because of a contract dispute.

The move enraged Holmgren and Favre especially, who couldn't understand why he picked that time to make his stand. Sharpe relented when he received assurances that his contract would be reworked, and he went out and played well, catching a touchdown amid a smattering of boos.

After the game, teammates again rolled their eyes, shrugged their shoulders and said, "That's Sterling." But it was different this time. This move was viewed as selfish and came at a point where the Packers were beginning to believe in themselves as a team ready to do something special. For the rest of the season, no one really knew what to expect from the mercurial receiver.

Favre knew Sharpe was his main weapon and continued to feed him all season, but the two would never see eye to eye again—if they ever had before.

But away from the prying eyes of fans and media and even teammates, Sharpe again proved he was a surprise. The man who shunned publicity and would not sign autographs in public did what no one expected.

Every Tuesday, the players' traditional day off during the season, Sharpe would arrive at the team headquarters at 7 a.m. and face boxes of letters, photos and memorabilia requesting autographs. Sharpe would sit in front of his locker and sign every one for as long as it took. That is the enigma that was Sterling Sharpe.

But the journey finally ended for him in 1994. Bothered by a neck injury all season as well as the toe problem, Sharpe continued to play and produce. But in the season finale in Tampa, Sharpe caught a pass, was tackled and briefly went numb.

After the game, it was learned that there was a narrowing in his spinal column that had always been there but was never noticed in any exams before. The choice was simple—if Sharpe continued to play, he risked permanent paralysis.

The news was a thunderbolt to the Packers and their fans, especially with a playoff game coming up against the Detroit Lions. But there was no choice to make. Sharpe's season ended then and there, and the Packers had to move on with life without their best receiver.

In February of 1995, the reality hit home even harder when the Packers released Sharpe due to the injury. He departed as the team's all-time leading receiver with 595 catches and second in yards with 8,134 and touchdowns with 65.

After struggling through the early awful years under coach Lindy Infante, Sharpe was released just as the Packers were on the cusp of greatness. In fact, just two years later, with Antonio Freeman as the lead receiver, the Packers won the Super Bowl, and Sharpe, who briefly considered a comeback in 1996, watched from afar as an ESPN analyst.

Unknowable and exasperating, Sharpe still remains one of the best and toughest receivers this franchise has ever known. And while he may never be loved as many ex-Packers are, he will always be respected. Which is all Sharpe really wanted anyway.

Good Times and Bad Times

To look at the Green Bay Packers organization today is to see a franchise at the top of its game. After nearly 20 years of stunning mediocrity, the Packers have not had a losing season since 1991. Since 1992, they have reached the playoffs eight times, winning four division titles and a Super Bowl along the way.

In a recent *ESPN The Magazine* survey, the Green Bay Packers were voted the top franchise in pro sports, and as far as NFL Properties marketing is concerned, the Packers remain one of the most popular teams in the NFL. And since 1960, the Packers have sold every game out and the waiting list for season tickets still stands at more than 50,000 names.

Today, a new $295 million renovation has been completed, making Lambeau Field one of the showpieces of the league while managing, at least in some measure, to retain the feel of the old stadium.

But while the Packers are riding high these days, it wasn't always that way. In fact, the franchise found itself in danger of dissolving altogether several times in its history.

Keep in mind that this is a franchise formed in 1919 on little more than the hope that it would evolve into something special. And those hopes didn't always translate into cold, hard cash on the barrelhead. For years, the team struggled to stay afloat financially, unsure almost from one game to the next where they'd find the money to keep going.

For example, in 1922, just three years after forming, Andrew Turnbull, the publisher of the *Press-Gazette*, formed the Green Bay Football Corporation to help keep the team going. Curly Lambeau, the legendary player and coach who helped form the team, was one of the buyers, purchasing the team back for $250 from the Acme Packing Company.

But the problems continued, and in 1935, Lee Joannes, the owner of several grocery stores in town, paid $10,000 out of his own pocket to pay off team debts.

But perhaps the biggest threat to the team's survival came in 1949-50 with the advent of the All-American Football League, which siphoned players away from the NFL and paid them more than many NFL teams could muster.

The Packers were no different, and they faced a dire economic situation. It got so bad that in 1949, they played an intrasquad game on Thanksgiving Day and charged $2 a ticket. The team raised close to $50,000 and managed to cobble together enough cash to finish the season.

The following year, the second of the Packers' growing tradition of stock sales was held. Charging $25 per share to anyone who wanted to own a piece of an NFL team, the Packers raised $118,000, which again allowed the team to stay in business.

Years earlier, the Packers knew they couldn't survive for long without the help of the rest of Wisconsin, so in 1932 they began to play some "home" games in Milwaukee, first at State Fair Park and then at Milwaukee County Stadium.

That continued through the 1994 season when it became clear that the Packers, ironically, were losing money playing football in what amounted to a 50,000-seat stadium designed for baseball.

The decision enraged Milwaukee-area season ticket holders who rightfully pointed out that the Packers might not exist without their help. In the end, the Packers struck a deal to give Milwaukee fans three games a year at Lambeau Field, and it's a policy that seems to have worked ever since.

Packers PR director Lee Remmel, a nearby Shawano, Wisconsin native who has followed the team for 58 years, first as a reporter for the *Press-Gazette* and then as the public relations director since 1974, has seen nearly every trial and tribulation this franchise has gone through.

He has watched the team dance on the edge of oblivion and escape every time for one simple reason.

"It's the can-do spirit of this community," he said. "When there has been a financial crisis, people have always responded. I think that's why the Packers have survived. It's been a very deep commitment. The people here are not going to give it up."

The New Lambeau Field

E ven today, the struggles to keep up with the rest of the NFL continue to bedevil the Packers, the only NFL franchise without a single owner.

"We have no deep pockets we can go to," president Bob Harlan said.

And Lambeau Field itself has been the source of the pride, concern, confusion and occasional anger about the continuing viability of this franchise.

Originally built in 1957 for the princely sum of $960,000 and called simply City Stadium, it seated just 32,000 fans, and no one knew the history and controversy it would cause.

In June, 1965, Curly Lambeau, the Green Bay native who not only helped found the team but kept it alive and then coached it through its first era of glory, died. It was decided soon after to rededicate the stadium and call it Lambeau Field in his honor.

The only problem was that coach Vince Lombardi, who had already led the Packers to two NFL titles and was on the verge of winning three more, didn't like the idea. In fact, he hated it.

If the stadium should be named for anyone, he thought, it should be named for him, because of what he'd accomplished right here and right now.

But Lombardi knew there was little he could do about it. As he quietly stewed, the plan went ahead. In time, he had the road running by Lambeau Field, formerly known as Highland Avenue, named for him.

It wasn't quite the same, but Lombardi received perhaps the ultimate honor years later when the trophy awarded to the Super Bowl champ would be renamed the Lombardi Trophy.

Meanwhile, Lambeau Field grew and expanded and changed while staying, in many respects, the same.

For years, the facility that hosted such epic games as the Ice Bowl in 1967, the Monday Night Madness in 1983 when the Packers outpointed the defending world champion Washington Redskins, and the 1996 NFC title game was big enough.

In the mid-1990s, the place held 59,000 fans and had enough luxury boxes to keep most of the local corporate bigwigs happy. But then the NFL began to change, and not necessarily for the better, as far as the Packers were concerned.

Nearly every NFL city had built a new stadium, was planning to build one or had a major renovation on the drawing board. From Cincinnati to Washington to Pittsburgh to Tampa, teams were building newer and larger stadiums and reaping the benefits from the increased revenue.

The Packers, however, hadn't looked that far down the road and hadn't really anticipated the building boom. By 1998, even though they were flush with success on the field after back-to-back Super Bowl appearances, the Packers were losing money for several reasons.

First, with the added success came the realization that they'd have to pay their players more money. Second, Lambeau Field wasn't generating enough revenue on its own since it was only used, at most, 12 times a year. And third, there was the familiar refrain that there was no filthy rich owner who could simply take money from one of his other companies and pump it into his football team.

"We were reaching a crisis situation," said team president Bob Harlan.

Over the course of several years in the late '90s, the Packers went from one of the most profitable teams in the NFL to the middle of the pack. And projections were ominous that if something wasn't done, they'd fall to the bottom of the league.

Without a competitive team, the reasoning went, they couldn't pay their players to stay and they wouldn't be able to attract the free agents necessary to stay competitive. The franchise would continue to hemorrhage money and, in the worst-case scenario, the franchise could fold.

Using that doomsday scenario, Harlan embarked on an ambitious plan to renovate Lambeau Field and make it competitive with every other team in the league.

Harlan had no idea how difficult the journey would be.

The plan called for a $295 million renovation that would keep the intimacy of the bowl structure that made Lambeau Field so unique.

"We asked engineers to test that bowl to see how long it would last," Harlan said. "When they told us it would last for another 50 years, we knew we wanted to renovate instead of building a new stadium. Our goal all along was to keep Lambeau Field as it was."

The project would include adding seats, new luxury boxes and club seats as well as building an atrium that would house a new Packers Pro Shop as well as a restaurant, retail store and banquet rooms that would stay open all year.

Harlan even recalled those wedding parties that for years had pulled into the Lambeau Field parking and posed for photos next to the historic stadium. Now, Harlan thought, those people could actually hold their wedding receptions right there in the stadium.

But somebody had to pay for the project, and when the state of Wisconsin determined it would only kick in a small amount to help with road construction and parking, Harlan knew the bitter pill would have to be swallowed by taxpayers.

In a shrewd bit of politicking, an independent accounting report stated that the Packers generated $144 million for Brown County, where the stadium is located. Using those numbers, the Packers announced the renovation would be paid for with a .05 percent sales tax in Brown County.

The word "tax" enraged many people who couldn't understand why they should have to help pay for a stadium they'd never have a chance to see up close. The Packers countered by saying that without a renovated stadium, the team would eventually slip away, and then Brown County would really have a problem.

For Harlan, who began in the Packers' organization working on contracts before eventually being named president, this became his consuming passion.

"I had no idea how difficult this would be," he said. And in more ways than one.

Harlan, along with his second in command, John Jones, spent hours, days and months in the state capital in Madison lobbying politicians for support. Then, with reluctant approval from lawmakers, Harlan and Jones had to convince Brown County residents, who would vote on the tax in a referendum in September of 2000.

Harlan was shocked when he saw poll numbers that suggested residents not only rejecting the tax, but rejecting it by a huge margin.

So Harlan went from door to door and house to house like an old-time politician, scrounging for votes.

"I remember going to a factory in Green Bay and going up and shaking people's hands and asking for their support," Harlan said. "And a lot of them would turn away from me and say, 'Don't you touch me. Are you crazy? What do you think you're doing?' It was very difficult."

The referendum was scheduled for a Tuesday, and Harlan, who never missed a Packers game home or away, decided to stay in Green Bay that Sunday when the Packers played (and lost) in Buffalo. He went to restaurants and churches and anywhere else he could think of to meet people and try to convince them of the need for this project.

In the end, the referendum did pass, 53 percent to 47 percent, and the project moved forward.

By the spring of 2002, the project was 70 percent complete and Harlan found himself driving around the new facility every day just to marvel at it and to remember what the battle was like.

"I get calls on occasion from people who had opposed it before and they say, 'You know, Bob, I've seen it and I like it,'" Harlan said. "Then they say, 'Maybe I was wrong.' But I don't look at it that way. We always respected everyone's opinion, but we really needed this and it's better than I ever imagined."

Finding a Coach

There was nothing left for Vince Lombardi to accomplish. He had taken over a flaccid Packers team in 1959 after it had gone the previous 11 years without a winning record and turned it into the most powerful, the most recognized, the most feared team in the NFL.

In nine seasons, he posted an 89-29-4 record and won five NFL titles, including the first two of those things that would come to be known as the Super Bowl. He was the best coach the NFL had ever seen, and if you didn't think so, all you had to do was ask him.

"We hated the SOB," center Ken Bowman said. "But he made us win."

And because of it, Lombardi would become part of the mythology of the NFL: the headmaster of the team that dominated everyone it played; that could win under the worst circumstances; that would run the vaunted "Packer Sweep" all day long and into the night until you found a way to stop it.

But while Lombardi knew where he fit into the pantheon of football gods, no one in Green Bay understood, because Lombardi never really let anybody in.

"He was a very complex individual," Packers longtime public relations director Lee Remmel said. "He didn't make much of an attempt to get to know people. He valued his privacy."

As a result, while Lombardi provided wins and notoriety for the place that would come to be known as

"Titletown," no one could break through to figure out what made the man tick.

Maybe that's why it came as no surprise to some that after the 1967 season, Lombardi decided he'd had enough of coaching and wanted to concentrate on his other duties as general manager. To his critics, the move smacked of a man bailing out just in time.

The players on those powerhouse teams that had made him a legend were getting older now. Some had already retired and others were nearing the end of their careers, and they knew it. So did Lombardi. And he was in no mood and no position in life to start over with mediocrity.

So some believed Lombardi kicked himself upstairs and left the rebuilding process to lifelong assistant and devoted Lombardi lieutenant, defensive coordinator Phil Bengston.

He never had a chance.

Trying to outrun Lombardi's considerable legacy was bad enough for Bengston, but he also had to live with the realization that staring down at him from the press box every Sunday was the legend himself.

"It was an impossible situation for him," Remmel said. "It would have been an impossible situation for anyone."

Bengston lasted three seasons, posted a 20-21-1 record and did not take the Packers to the playoffs. He resigned soon after the third season ended.

Meanwhile, the coaching bug, not to mention a staggering financial commitment from the Washington Redskins, brought Lombardi back to the sidelines in 1969. He coached one season for the Redskins and led them to their best record in 20 years before he died of colon cancer on September 3, 1970.

With Bengston's resignation at the end of the 1970 season, a new and extended dark age began for the Packers.

First Dan Devine tried to revive the team's fortunes, but he could only manage 25 wins in four seasons, even though the Packers did have a brief renaissance when they won the NFC Central title in 1972.

Next came the return of the icon, former quarterback legend Bart Starr. And even though he had no head coaching experience anywhere, in the eyes of hungry and desperate Packers fans, he didn't need any.

"This was Bart Starr," said former center Larry McCarren, a 12th-round draft pick in 1973. "Bart Starr. He was everything."

So popular was Starr that fans formed a line two deep outside the Packers' locker room down the Lambeau Field parking lot to the practice field just to watch Starr pass by.

In nine seasons, he again took the Packers to one playoff berth and put together an offense that was exciting and explosive, but the overall results remained disappointing as he posted a 53-77-3 record.

As the Packers again reached to the past with another former star, legendary right tackle Forrest Gregg, who came to the Packers from the Cincinnati Bengals, nothing really changed as he won just 25 games in four seasons.

The frustration level grew exponentially as Gregg resigned in 1988 to take over as head coach at his alma mater, Southern Methodist University.

Faced with an opportunity to make a big splash with a head coach who could steer the Packers back toward respectability, they set their sights on one of the hottest college coaches in the land, Michigan State's George Perles.

Perles had just come off leading the Spartans to a Rose Bowl berth, and he had the pedigree the Packers wanted— he was a former defensive coordinator with the Pittsburgh Steelers and a guy who knew what it took to win in the NFL.

Gregg resigned January 15, and the Packers leaped almost immediately on Perles and a deal was worked out quickly.

With everything seemingly in place and a public announcement imminent, Bob Harlan, who was then working in the public relations office, called Perles with some housekeeping details.

"I said, 'George, I need a few quotes from you for our press release,' and Perles said, 'Bob, I'm not coming,'" Harlan said.

Stunned, Harlan said, "Who else have you told?" and Perles said he'd told no one off campus. Still, word had already leaked out locally and nationally that Perles was the Packers' choice as their next head coach, and Harlan had to deliver the word to the team executives that it was off.

"That was probably the low point for this franchise," he said.

Harlan never really knew if Perles backed out because he received a better offer from Michigan State (which was likely the case) or if the thought of taking over a moribund franchise like Green Bay was just too much to handle. Whatever it was, the Packers were left in the lurch, and they were embarrassed. Again.

Forced to shift gears quickly, the Packers went to their No. 2 choice, Cleveland Browns offensive coordinator Lindy Infante, who had already been told he wasn't getting the job. But when the Packers came back to him, helmet in hand, so to speak, he jumped at the opportunity.

In four seasons, Infante was 24-40 and was fired at the end of the 1991 season when new general manager Ron Wolf came on board and decided massive changes were needed.

That move marked the end of the dry spell, though no one knew it at the time.

Monday Night Madness

It may not have been the greatest game in team history, but it certainly was the most fun. Remember?

It was a brisk October 17 night in 1983 and *Monday Night Football* made its way to Lambeau Field for a rare appearance. And what a sellout crowd, as well as a stunned national TV audience saw, was something no one will forget any time soon.

"I probably still get three or four people asking me about that game every week," team president Bob Harlan said. "It was unbelievable."

The game pitted the visiting Washington Redskins, the defending Super Bowl champs and on pace to set a league record for most points scored in a season, against the Packers, who would go on to set a club record for points scored that would stand up for 13 years.

"We started that season lighting it up," Pro Bowl center Larry McCarren said of an offense that featured Lynn Dickey at quarterback (who threw for 4,458 yards and 29 touchdowns) and a receiving corps of wide receivers

James Lofton and John Jefferson and tight end Paul Coffman, who combined for 169 catches and 26 touchdowns.

The problem was, as mercurial as the offense was in averaging 386 yards a game and scoring 429 points for the season, the defense was horrendous.

Green Bay's defense was really a defense only in the academic sense, as it put 11 guys on the field, though not many were able to stop anybody. It got to the point where the offense, which could strike quickly and from anywhere on the field, had to go more conservative as the season progressed just to keep the woeful defense off the field.

But prior to the Redskins game, offensive coordinator Bob Schnelker decided to throw the conservatism out the window. In a meeting with the offense prior to the game, his advice was simple: Go out, have fun, score some points and let the defense fend for itself.

What resulted was the highest-scoring Monday night game in history and easily the most entertaining. McCarren recalled that the scoring was so constant and the action so unrelenting that the crowd had no time to sit back and take a breath.

"There's usually a din you can hear at Lambeau Field, and the volume increases every time we crack a big run," he said. "That night, it was a constant din. No one could really sit back and relax."

In the end, it was Jan Stenerud's 20-yard field goal with 54 seconds remaining that put the Packers on top to stay. Still, Washington had a chance to win on the final play, but Mark Moseley's 39-yard field goal attempt sailed wide, causing Redskins quarterback and Moseley's holder, Joe Theismann, to look back at his friend and say in exasperation, "You've got to be kidding me."

The final score? Packers 48, Redskins 47. It was a game that saw the two teams combine for 1,025 total yards of offense, including 771 through the air. And Dickey was superb, completing 22 of 31 passes for 387 yards and three touchdowns.

When it was over, hundreds of fans hung around Lambeau Field, soaking in the victory and not quite understanding what they'd seen.

"They just wouldn't leave," Harlan said. "I'm not sure what they were waiting around for, but they knew they just didn't want to go."

"To this day, people still talk about that game," McCarren said. "As far as Packer moments go, it's my favorite."

The Rivalry

No doubt the first elbow to the mouth came in that first game between the Green Bay Packers and Chicago Bears. Knowing these two teams, it probably came on the first play of the first game. It has always been ever thus between the Packers and Bears, a rivalry that many believe remains the best in all of pro sports.

It has had its ups and downs, to be sure. There would be times when the Packers would dominate the proceedings as recently as, well, these days, having won 16 of the last 18 meetings between the two teams. Prior to that, the Bears controlled the series, winning 10 of 11 at one point in the 1980s.

Maybe that's why it's been such a great rivalry over the 164 times the two teams have met—it's because nothing is ever guaranteed. And the names have been the stuff of legend and the Hall of Fame.

Coaches like George Halas and Mike Ditka, Vince Lombardi and Curly Lambeau. Players like Ray Nitschke and Dick Butkus, Walter Payton and Paul Hornung, Jim McMahon and Brett Favre. It is, and as always has been, the stuff of high drama from the earliest days when these two teams first collided.

For years, the rivalry was always hard-fought, rarely clean, but at least respectful within the context of what pro football was. But something changed in the mid-1980s when the Bears were beginning their rise to greatness and the Packers were still looking for some direction. In particular, the rivalry grew its nastiest when Ditka was coaching the Bears and Forrest Gregg ran the Packers.

Maybe it stemmed from ancient wars between the two men when they collided with each other as players, or perhaps it was a personality clash. Whatever it was, the games in that period were some of the ugliest ever played.

"I don't think the rivalry was ever as full of antics as it was in that period," former Packers linebacker Brian Noble said. "We weren't a very good team, but if we could beat the Bears, it made our season."

The spark may well have been lit in 1985 when the Bears, on their way to winning the Super Bowl, steamrolled the Packers. In a Bears win at Lambeau Field, Ditka even let his 380-pound defensive tackle, William "Refrigerator" Perry, line up at tailback, take a handoff and plow over linebacker George Cumby for a one-yard touchdown that added insult to considerable injury.

The following season it got even worse when Packers defensive end Charles Martin came equipped with a towel

Quarterback Lynn Dickey (left) and center Larry McCarren were key elements in helping trigger one of the NFL's most prolific offenses in the early 1980s. *Photo courtesy of Vernon J. Biever*

that had the numbers of five Bears he hoped to disable that day. He got his chance.

In a game at Soldier Field, Bears quarterback Jim McMahon had long since unloaded a pass when Martin ran up, picked up McMahon and threw him to the ground. As McMahon lay prostrate on the ground, Martin rejoiced over him, enraging not only Bears fans and players and fans around the league, but even a few Packers as well.

"I thought those guys [the Bears] would try to kill every one of us after that," Noble said.

Then there was the late hit by Green Bay cornerback Ken Stills on Matt Suhey a full 10 seconds after the play had ended. There were other incidents, overt and otherwise, that more resembled schoolyard bullies on a playground as opposed to pro football players.

Football had degenerated into pro wrestling, and it was doing nothing for the reputation of either team, or, for that matter, the league.

After the 1986 scrum in Soldier Field, Packers executive Bob Harlan was walking past the Bears' locker room when Suhey came up to him.

"Bob," he said simply, "this has got to change."

Harlan agreed.

"That era was an embarrassment to this franchise," he said.

Noble had seen enough as well and went to the Bears' locker room after the game to apologize to the players and Ditka. As he reached their locker room, security guards stopped him and asked what he wanted. After he identified himself, the guards still denied him access.

That's when Ditka's wife, Diana, showed up and told the guards to get out of the way and let him through.

Rugged linebacker Brian Noble fought through nine often lousy seasons with the Packers. *Photo courtesy of Vernon J. Biever*

Ditka was sitting in his office when Noble came in and told him how sorry he was for the Packers' actions.

"Don't worry about it," Ditka said. "We'll get it straightened out. Just keep doing what you're doing."

And even though he saw his share of these wars over the years and knew how volatile they could be, Noble believes the fury of the rivalry then might have been overstated just a little.

"Sure it was a great rivalry and you knew anything could happen," he said. "But I got along with all of their guys. They appreciated the way I played the game and I appreciated how they played it."

Forrest and Dan

They were two coaches who could not have been any different if they'd been born on different planets.

There was the professorial Dan Devine, who faced the unenviable task of trying to rebuild a Packers franchise still longing for the days of Vince Lombardi and wondering why no one could provide them.

Then there was Forrest Gregg, the tough-as-leather former offensive guard who tried to instill old-school football into a team in an era where that was no longer fashionable.

Neither had much success turning the Packers around, but they made life interesting while they were there.

Devine came to the Packers in 1971 to replace Phil Bengston, who had sputtered in three years trying to replace the legendary Lombardi.

Maybe it should have been an omen of things to come when, in Devine's regular-season opener as Green Bay's head coach, he was run over on the sidelines in a game against the New York Giants at Lambeau Field and suffered a broken leg.

Those Packers were a transitional team that still had some pieces from the glory years like wide receiver Carroll Dale, a fading Bart Starr, safety Willie Wood and linebacker Dave Robinson as well as newcomers like tight end Rich McGeorge and cornerback Ken Ellis. As a result, the Packers staggered in with a 4-8-2 record, the franchise's worst since 1958.

The next season, with a revamped lineup and philosophy that emphasized running the ball before anything else, the Packers shocked themselves and the NFL by posting a 10-4 record and winning the NFC Central Division for the first time since 1967. It was a strange team that averaged just 253 yards a game on offense, 162 of which came on the ground.

The studs were a pair of 220-pound running backs, John Brockington and MacArthur Lane, who for the times were behemoths. Brockington ran for 1,027 yards that season and Lane added 821.

"It really didn't matter who we handed the ball to," center Ken Bowman said. "We could move the ball on anybody."

It was a good thing they could run the ball, because Devine had little confidence in his quarterback, Scott Hunter, who somehow led the Packers to a division title while completing just 43 percent of his passes and throwing six touchdown passes.

Devine recalled at the time how he'd keep Hunter in line late in a game.

"I'd call a timeout and bring Scott over to the sidelines," Devine recalled. "I'd tell him to take off his helmet and look me straight in the eye. Then I'd tell him: 'Scott, the only way we can lose this game is if you screw up.' Then I'd send him back to the huddle."

It was classic Devine, a psychology major in college who never failed to use whatever was necessary to get the job done.

"He was different," center Larry McCarren said. "We'd be in team meetings and then he'd flip off the projector after a mistake and there'd be a pregnant pause. That's when we knew someone was going to get it. But he knew what it took to win."

Unfortunately for Devine, he couldn't translate that to his team.

That 1972 season ended with a first-round playoff loss to the Washington Redskins, who employed an eight-man defensive front to stop the Packers' vaunted running game.

What seemed like a turn in fortunes, though, was just a cruel hoax. The Packers tumbled back to 5-7-2 the next season and 6-8 the year after that, and Devine, who was always believed to have one foot out of Green Bay anyway, departed to take the head coaching job at Notre Dame.

Fast forward nine years. Bart Starr, who led the Packers to one playoff appearance but little else, resigned and was replaced by another icon from the championship years, former right tackle Forrest Gregg.

With his Texas drawl and fiery personality, he was a different animal from both the studious Devine and the more laconic Starr.

Dan Devine and his professorial manner as a head coach endeared him to some players and infuriated others. *Photo courtesy of Vernon J. Biever*

"He was as upfront as any coach I'd ever had," said linebacker Brian Noble, a fifth-round draft pick in 1985, Gregg's second season as head coach. "He was honest. If he had a problem with you, you knew he had a problem with you. That might have offended some people, but I'd rather have a coach do that than smile at you and then cut you the next week."

Gregg was still old-school. He played under Lombardi and he had succeeded under Lombardi and his dictatorial style. He then took that style with him and eventually whipped the Cincinnati Bengals into the 1981 Super Bowl, where they lost to San Francisco.

But the game was changing, and Gregg wasn't necessarily changing with it.

"He couldn't understand how players didn't make the commitment to the game anymore," Noble said.

Noble recalled a story that summed up Gregg's approach.

"It was the Monday after a loss and we were looking at film from the game," he said. "Forrest is twitching away and he's lambasting us. Then he focuses on Alphonso Carreker, Tom Flynn and Donnie Humphrey and he says in his way, 'You guys remind me a lot of fat cows standing in the shade chewing your cud.' I was a rookie, and I thought I was playing pretty well, and I snickered at that. Forrest looked down at me and said, 'And you, you're nothing but a low-life scum-of-the-earth worm rookie. In our opinion, you don't even exist.' I stopped laughing."

That was the same year a fight broke out between coaches and players in the locker room after an especially tough loss.

He was a Hall of Fame player under Vince Lombardi and a Super Bowl coach in Cincinnati, but Forrest Gregg knew little but frustration as Green Bay's head coach from 1984-87. *Photo courtesy of Vernon J. Biever*

"We had just gotten hammered," Noble said. "We gave up like 260 yards rushing or something like that and it was a terrible. Forrest came in and yelled at us."

In the center of the locker room was a garbage can full of ice that held soft drinks. Gregg was so mad, he kicked the garbage can and, because it was so full of melted ice, it didn't budge.

"You knew it had to hurt," Noble said.

As several players stifled laughs, Gregg verbally attacked linebacker Mike Douglass for what he considered especially poor play. Douglass yelled back, then Gregg yelled back, and before long, soda cans and bodies were flying back and forth before order was restored.

"I was stunned," Noble said. "Here I am winning for most of my career and then I'm here and I'm seeing this. I just put my head down and said, 'This is hell.'"

Gregg began to think the same thing before too long, and after two more seasons of losing football, he resigned to take over as head coach at his alma mater, Southern Methodist University.

The Quarterback, Part III

He was going to be the next great thing in the Green Bay Packers' illustrious history. With his flowing blonde locks and rapscallion personality, Don Majkowski was everything desperate Packers fans had waited for after years of stunning mediocrity.

He even had the perfect nickname—he was "Majic." He was the "Majic Man," a fan of the rock group Guns 'n' Roses, and he was going to deliver the Packers back to the promised land.

Green Bay's 10th-round draft in 1987 out of the University of Virginia, he split time that first season with Randy Wright as the Packers limped in with a 5-9-1 record that sent Forrest Gregg scurrying toward a college coaching job at SMU.

The next season, under new coach Lindy Infante, who boasted a philosophy of throw first and ask questions later, Majkowski saw more playing time, though injuries and inconsistency saw him again split time with Wright. It was another lost season as Green Bay went a ludicrous 4-12.

Finally in 1989, Wright was gone and the job belonged to Majkowski free and clear. Little did anyone realize, especially after an opening-game 23-31 loss to New Orleans at Lambeau Field, that it would be a season to remember.

Over the course of the next four months, the Packers, with Majkowski at the controls, would take fans on a wild ride of last-second wins, crushing losses and the kind of heroics that reminded many of the great years in the 1960s.

It was an unforgettable, agitating season that saw the Packers win 10 games, though seven came by four points or fewer and four of those were by one point. The highlight was certainly the November 5 game at Lambeau Field against the hated Bears. In a game that perhaps only rivals the Ice Bowl in terms of fond memories for Packers fans, Majkowski directed a frantic last-minute drive that stalled at the Chicago nine.

Finally, on fourth down, Majkowski rolled right and desperately looked for anyone to throw to. Wide receiver

Sterling Sharpe broke open in the end zone and Majkowski found him for the apparent touchdown and the win.

But the line judge threw a penalty flag to signify that Majkowski had crossed the line of scrimmage. The play was nullified and, with the loss of down, the game apparently went to the Bears. But that was before instant replay, still in its infancy in the NFL, got involved.

Wanting to review the play to make sure, the powers that be decided, after a five-minute delay, that Majkowski had not crossed the line. The touchdown was good and the touchdown stood, sending Lambeau Field into convulsions.

"That was the most emotional I'd ever been in my career to that point," said linebacker Brian Noble, who had never beaten the Bears in his four seasons.

The Bears, of course, furiously objected, and further replays seemed to suggest that Majkowski had indeed been in violation. But there was nothing anyone could do at that stage. And for years, Packers fans reveled in the game, sending faxes to Chicago area radio hosts that said simply, "After further review, the Bears still suck."

And the architect of it all was Majkowski, the swashbuckler who threw for 4,318 yards and 27 touchdowns that season and was voted to the Pro Bowl. The only negative for the Packers, and it was a substantial one, was that due to tiebreakers, the Packers missed the playoffs despite tying Minnesota for the division title. Today, of course, with the expanded playoff format, the Packers would have qualified. But then, there was only one wild card and the Packers were left out in the cold.

Nonetheless, there was reason for optimism the next season. Majkowski was a young stud of a quarterback who was only going to get better, and the future looked promising for the Packers.

"That 1989 season was the first year I believed we could win any game we got into," Noble said. "No one wanted to play us."

Indeed, Majkowski could have owned Green Bay, and most of Wisconsin, if he wanted to. He was a dream for product endorsement that included a huge billboard along Highway 41, the main road from the Upper Peninsula of Michigan to Milwaukee, that showed a smiling Majkowski as he hawked a local car dealership.

But sometimes fame can turn ugly. Understanding that the Packers' fortunes rode on his right arm, Majkowski engaged in a nasty and protracted contract holdout as training camp 1990 began.

These were the days before salary caps and signing bonuses and prorated deals. The Packers could play hardball with Majkowski and they did. So the holdout dragged through training camp and into the season, and all that early optimism from fans turned toward anger— not only toward the Packers and their hard-line policy, but toward Majkowski as well.

Meanwhile a young quarterback named Anthony Dilweg stepped into the vacuum and took over as the starter. He performed superbly in the season opener, throwing three touchdown passes in a 36-24 win over the Los Angeles Rams, and was named NFC Offensive Player of the Week.

But Majkowski saw the writing on the wall, knew his position as the savior was slipping away, and he ended his holdout.

It wasn't the same. He took back his starting spot in the third game of the season, a stultifying 17-3 loss to Kansas City. He'd start eight games and the Packers would win four, but the magic, so to speak, of the previous season had evaporated. In a November 18 game against the Phoenix Cardinals, Majkowski separated his shoulder and was lost for the season. The season collapsed from there as Green Bay dropped its last five games and finished 6-10.

"We were so optimistic after 1989," said team president Bob Harlan, who was admittedly swept up in the euphoria and, unwisely as it turned out, extended Infante's contract.

It only got worse the next season when Majkowski, again plagued by injury and inconsistency, played only nine games, threw eight interceptions and just three touchdown passes and the Packers skidded to a 4-12 season that cost Infante his job.

In another twist that would prove to be prophetic for this franchise, Mike Holmgren, another offensive genius who had worked wonders in San Francisco with some quarterback named Joe Montana, was named the new head coach, and clearly Don Majkowski was not part of his plan.

The Packers had given up a first-round draft pick for some kid wasting away on the Atlanta Falcons bench named Brett Favre. He was raw but full of potential, and new general manager Ron Wolf had staked his reputation that Favre would be the quarterback of the future for the Packers.

Holmgren was intrigued too, but he also knew Favre wasn't ready to come in and start right away. So he went with Majkowski because, frankly, he had no one else. After an opening-game overtime loss to Minnesota, the Packers went to Tampa the next week and were destroyed by the Bucs, 31-3. In that game, Holmgren inserted Favre just to see what he could do, and the results weren't pretty. Actually, the first pass Favre ever completed was to himself, when, under a huge pass rush, his first NFL pass was tipped and he grabbed it.

Then came the game that would take its place comfortably in Packers legend.

In a home game against the Cincinnati Bengals, Majkowski suffered a sprained ankle in the first quarter and was replaced by Favre. The word among press box types even then was that Holmgren might have sprained Majkowski's ankle himself just to find the opportunity to play Favre. A cynical perspective or not, Holmgren was anxious to get his new young quarterback into the game, and the results are there for all to see.

Favre was all over the map in that game, calling formations that did not exist and throwing balls to receivers who weren't open. But his rocket arm and gunslinger mentality made plays out of nothing, and he quickly won over the Lambeau Field crowd.

And those fans he didn't have in the beginning were certainly his at the end of the game when he threw a game-winning touchdown pass to Kitrick Taylor with 13 seconds to play.

"I never even saw it," Favre said at the time. "I just threw it up there and waited for the cheers."

Favre had the youthful exuberance that made him irresistible, and he had the swagger Majkowski had featured only three years ago. The difference was that Favre had more innate talent than Majkowski, and he would do anything to get the Packers a victory.

He was the "Majik Man"—at least for one season. Don Majkowski had a superb 1989 season, but injuries and inconsistency ended his reign almost before it started. His injured ankle early in the 1992 season allowed Brett Favre to take over as quarterback, and, well, you know the rest of the story. *Photo courtesy of Vernon J. Biever*

"He's like a linebacker who plays quarterback," center James Campen said at the time. He had no idea how prophetic those words were.

The next week, Favre started against Pittsburgh, and he has started every game since through the 2002 season—regular season and playoffs—a record never likely to be touched in NFL annals.

Majkowski? He was gone the following season, turning up later in Detroit but never again reaching the level he did in that magical 1989 season.

The Guy from California

Mike Holmgren was a coach in demand in the winter of 1991. He was the flavor of the month, the next great coaching prospect, the man every struggling franchise needed to turn their wayward teams around. And he was the coach Ron Wolf set his gaze on from the minute he accepted the general manager's job in Green Bay.

There had been a brief flirtation with longtime friend and ex-New York Giants head Bill Parcells, but Wolf wanted Holmgren and he never made any bones about it.

"He's the best coach out there," Wolf told team president Bob Harlan.

And Harlan, who had given Wolf unfettered power to do whatever was necessary to turn the Packers around, told his newest employee to do whatever was necessary to secure his services.

But the Packers weren't the only team looking for a new head coach. The New York Jets were also looking, as were the Minnesota Vikings and several other teams, and Holmgren was set to make the rounds of every team just to see who had the most to offer.

But deep down, there was something about Green Bay that intrigued him. Holmgren had been a life-long student of football. He was a historian of the game with a keen appreciation of who and what had come before. And no one can be a student of football without flipping through the chapters about the Green Bay Packers.

Though California born and bred, he knew all about the Lombardi Packers and what they meant to pro football. He knew at least a little about Packers fans as well. He knew how special they were and how devoted they were to the team. He knew it would be a fishbowl in which to perform, but he also knew that if he were to succeed, what better place could he do it than Green Bay?

Maybe that's why the courtship was so short. Wolf knew he wanted Holmgren, and Holmgren knew he wanted the Packers, and the only way it wouldn't work would be if Wolf was an autocratic bully with whom he simply couldn't work. That proved not to be the case, and on Jan. 11, 1992, Holmgren was named head coach of the Packers.

The future had begun. One more time.

One of Holmgren's first, and fondest, memories of what his days in Green Bay would be like came when he went on a simple trip to the grocery store. Though still relatively unknown to most Packers fans, an elderly lady did recognize him and walked up with a simple but firm message: "OK, California, let's kick some butt."

It was a statement Holmgren took with him through his eight successful, if sometimes turbulent, years with the Packers.

He was a man with an immense ego, and even he would admit that. But it wasn't without reason. He was a coach bred to be successful, a man who knew from his earliest days that coaching was what he wanted, what he expected, to do.

As a young high school coach, he would often leave his wife and small children alone while he headed off to another coaching clinic somewhere to learn something else he didn't know before. And everything he picked up over the years went back into the game he'd devoted his life to.

But it wasn't until he hooked on with Bill Walsh and the San Francisco 49ers that Holmgren's stock as a hotshot young coach truly began to take root. Maybe it was because of his pedigree or perhaps it was because of how he worked with a pair of quarterbacks in San Francisco known as Joe Montana and Steve Young. Whatever it was, in the early 1990s, he was easily the hottest NFL coaching prospect in the land.

But even after he established himself in Green Bay and the success began to come, it was never a bargain dealing with Holmgren or his very specific ways of doing things.

"He wasn't a particularly warm man," said a longtime official in the organization. "He didn't have a great sense of humor."

But then came the addendum, as always—"He knew how to win, though."

Holmgren detested wasted time and energy. He craved perfection and attention to detail, just as his mentor, Bill Walsh, had. If a receiver was supposed to run an eight-yard hitch, it was eight yards and not seven and a half. If a quarterback was supposed to put a pass a foot in front of a receiver, it was a foot—nothing more and nothing less.

He had no use for players who fumbled the football, and he would send them to the bench or even release them as he did when he took over the Seattle Seahawks several years ago and couldn't abide the fumbling of his young tailback, Ahman Green. So frustrated did Holmgren become with him that he traded the promising back to Green Bay, where he's become a Pro Bowler.

Injuries, especially nagging little hurts, also sent Holmgren into a black rage. One year late in training camp, nearly 20 players were on the sidelines with every injury imaginable from a sore foot to a pulled hamstring to a jammed finger. Furious that so many so-called tough guys were sidelined with so many piddling injuries, he decided to make a point.

The next day in practice, Holmgren forced all the injured players to watch practice while wearing pink vests with huge white crosses on them. If they were going to sit out, Holmgren figured, the thousands of fans who lined the fences every day to watch were going to see it too.

The gag amused some players, angered others and made a few realize that maybe they weren't hurt so badly after all so that they made speedier recoveries. But that was one of the reasons Holmgren was so successful. It may not have been the popular way, but it was the way that worked for him.

Until, of course, the day that it didn't. And that may have started as early as Super Bowl week 1998 when the Packers were overwhelming favorites to beat the Denver Broncos in Super Bowl XXXII in San Diego.

The Packers were clearly the best team in the NFL that season, having rung up a 13-3 record. In fact, general manager Ron Wolf and many longtime NFL observers thought this was a stronger, deeper and better team than the Super Bowl-winning team of the year before. And several Packers believed it, too, which ultimately may have been their downfall.

With precious little to write about prior to the game, the germ of a story blossomed into a full-scale controversy when it was reported that Holmgren was interested in adding the title of general manager to his coaching duties. And Holmgren had indeed said, months earlier in an interview, that someday he'd like to do both jobs.

But in this setting and at this time, the relatively innocuous remark took on a life of its own, especially when Holmgren refused to deny he had an interest. Already it was being floated that Holmgren wanted to return to the Bay Area to run his beloved 49ers even though they already had a coach, Holmgren's protégé, Steve Mariucci, and a general manager.

The Seattle Seahawks were believed to have an interest, and the deep pockets, to perhaps lure the Packers coach, even though they, too, already had a coach and GM in place.

The furor eventually overwhelmed the Packers and Holmgren, and while they didn't play poorly against the Broncos, they were still upset, 31-24. Adding to the ruckus was Holmgren's admission that he had ordered his defense late in the game to allow Broncos back Terrell Davis to score a touchdown so that the Packers could get the ball back and try to score. It almost worked, too, as the Packers reached the Denver 31 before the drive stalled in the final seconds.

But it was another decision Holmgren had to defend to people he didn't feel the need to answer to.

Maybe that's why the 1998 season just didn't feel the same for Packers fans or, for that matter, Holmgren and his players.

A long home winning streak was shattered that season by the Minnesota Vikings. In a Monday night game in Pittsburgh, the Packers were awful. In Tampa, injuries all but decimated them. And then there was the verbal exchange with the fan at Lambeau Field during an uninspiring win over the hopeless Philadelphia Eagles.

The Packers still posted a solid 11-5 record and went to the playoffs for the sixth straight year, but a last-second loss in San Francisco brought the season to a crushing end.

And all the questions, all the uncertainty, all the rumors finally came to a boil as, less than a week after the season ended, Holmgren took over as head coach and general manager of the Seahawks.

Another era was over. Was a new one waiting?

On the Receiving End

R obert Brooks was one of those Packers receivers you could never quite get a handle on. He was, in fact, a study in contradictions.

Fiercely competitive, he was also vocal, sometimes to the point of annoyance, about his religion. A superbly well-conditioned athlete, he saw his career cut short by a succession of injuries. A player who professed no real interest in money, he nonetheless lobbied loud and long when it came to a new contract.

But Robert Brooks produced. When he was healthy, and that was really only one full season in his seven-year career, he was breathtaking. But he battled and fought and played through the kind of pain and injury that would have ended, almost before they started, the careers of other players.

Brooks was another of those well-documented and heralded "finds" by general manager Ron Wolf. He was a third-round selection of the Packers in 1992, the first Packers draft of Wolf and coach Mike Holmgren. He possessed superb speed and broke many of the college receiving records at South Carolina set by current Packer Sterling Sharpe. But whereas Sharpe was built to take punishment at the expense of a little extra speed, Brooks was slighter, a guy who could elude the big hit with his quickness and then make a defense pay with his speed.

And make no mistake, in those early days of the Holmgren regime, this was still Sharpe's team because he was the only receiver who had proved he could make plays on a consistent basis. For the first two years, while Brooks watched, that's the way it stayed, too.

But in 1994, Brooks began to assert himself and show that he could be a receiver to count on as well. He moved into the flanker spot opposite from Sharpe's at split end, and they became a devastating combo with Sharpe's tenacity and toughness and Brooks's speed. Sharpe again led the Packers that season with 94 catches, but Brooks was right up there too, with 58 receptions. No one figured Brooks would become a No. 1 receiver, but he never really needed to be with Sharpe in the picture.

But events soon changed and brought Brooks into the limelight far more than he ever wanted or probably expected.

It was at the end of the '94 season, just prior to the Packers' playoff game with Detroit, that it was announced Sharpe would miss the rest of the season with a neck injury. Suddenly, Brooks was the man.

But it figured to only be temporary. Sharpe would return the following season and all would be back to normal. Except, of course, that it wasn't. Sharpe's injury proved to be career-ending and the Packers were forced to cut their losses and release him.

And heading into the 1995 season, one of the biggest questions regarding the team was how Brooks would fill the suddenly massive vacuum.

To make matters seemingly worse, Brooks was diagnosed the spring before that season with a heart problem. The electrical impulses that keep the heart pumping apparently were, in a sense, short-circuiting in Brooks. He had never experienced a problem or any symptoms with it, but a routine physical discovered the problem and he went in for a minor heart "procedure" to fix it.

Declaring himself fit and ready, the questions still remained about a lead wide receiver who had heart surgery and was still essentially an unknown quantity. But those questions were answered soon enough.

In a week two Monday night game in Chicago, Brooks electrified the fans, his team and the country by gathering in a Favre pass at midfield and outrunning two defenders for a 99-yard touchdown that led to a Packers victory.

It was a play that said it all and showed, maybe, that Brooks could do the job after all.

The physical skills were clearly apparent, but he still demonstrated off the field that he had some work to do.

Perhaps he was taking a cue from his former teammate Sharpe, who had a well-known and long-lasting feud with the media.

For example, Brooks had agreed to be a co-host for a season-long local radio show, but after one week, he suddenly decided not to show up. He never even contacted the host, who was informed of the player's decision through the media relations department. That forced the radio host to scramble for a new co-host, a No. 3 tight end.

In the locker room, Brooks would blow hot and cold with the reporters who regularly covered the team. One day, he'd be expansive, funny and thoughtful, but the next he'd blow by a reporter without even a second look.

As well, he would challenge reporters to read the Bible and come back the next day quoting a passage before he'd grant an interview. Needless to say, many interviews never got done.

In 1995, Brooks had perhaps as good a season as a wide receiver could have. He caught 102 passes, averaged nearly 15 yards a catch and scored 13 touchdowns. In the NFC title game loss to Dallas, he caught two touchdown passes, including a 73-yarder, and almost single-handedly kept the Packers in the game.

He was on his way to a similar season in 1996 when disaster struck and altered his career forever.

On the first play of the Monday night game against San Francisco at Lambeau Field in October, Brooks locked up with cornerback Tyronne Drakeford on a simple block he'd executed a thousand times before. But somehow, as Drakeford pushed Brooks down, his body torqued awkwardly and twisted his right knee and the knee, in essence, came apart.

He tore the anterior cruciate ligament and ruptured the patellar tendon, and his season was over. The Packers eventually adapted that season and won the Super Bowl, but many players said the joy was tempered by the fact that Brooks could not share in the win.

But Brooks vowed to return, and he went back to his native South Carolina and resumed a rigorous training regiment that left teammates astounded. Brooks came back the following season and declared that his knee, and his psyche, were in one piece.

Still, the Packers faced a tough decision. They could either bring back Brooks, a longtime veteran who had proven himself time and again, or they could re-sign Andre Rison, the onetime troubled soul who seemed to have found a home in Green Bay and who had been so unselfish during the Super Bowl run.

They wanted both, but they could only keep one due to salary cap constraints. In the end, the Packers gambled and stayed with Brooks, signing him to a five-year, $15 million extension. Rison was heartbroken and made it clear that he thought the Packers had made a huge mistake.

But Brooks seemed ready again to prove the critics wrong. In fact, in the season opener, Brooks caught a touchdown pass, pointed to the knee and then pointed heavenward. He was back.

Brooks left no doubt that he thought he was worth the money the Packers invested in him, but he made one of the truly insightful comments about athletes and money that you're likely to hear.

"It's just money, man," he said one day. "You just use it to buy stuff. Then you realize you have too much stuff and you realize you don't need it anymore."

He caught 60 passes for 1,010 yards and seven touchdowns, but those who had watched Brooks blaze down the field in years past could see a difference. That extra gear that receivers need to run away from defenders was gone. He'd still get open and he'd still make the tough catch, but instead of separating himself, he was caught and dragged down. There was a hitch in his run as well that hadn't been there before, and though Brooks tried to deny it, even casual observers could see he was no longer the receiver he'd been prior to the devastating injury.

In 1998 he tried again, but more injuries knocked him back and he managed just 31 receptions. Meanwhile, he could only watch his understudy, Antonio Freeman, take over exactly the way he had done when Sharpe went down four years earlier. Freeman went on to catch 84 passes for a league-best 1,424 yards and 14 touchdowns that he parlayed into what at the time was the biggest contract in NFL history.

Brooks returned to training camp in 1999, but after the first day of practice he could already tell that whatever had been there before was gone.

The next day, he called a press conference and announced his retirement. It was a career that started quietly, flashed brilliantly but briefly, and then was over again. But Brooks was one of the lucky ones; at least he had his moment, and that's more than most players can say.

The Three Amigos

They came from different parts of the country, enjoyed different things, looked at life oh-so-differently, and generally could not have been more different if they'd tried. Which, come to think of it, they often did.

Yet, for a few years, quarterback Brett Favre, center Frank Winters and tight end Mark Chmura were as close, maybe closer, than brothers and became synonymous with real companionship and what it means to be teammates.

Favre, of course, came from the bayous of deepest Mississippi in a town called Kiln, which was close to a real backwater known as Rotten Springs.

Chmura, the Packers' Pro Bowl tight end in the early to mid-1990s, was from Deerfield, Mass. and went to Boston College.

Winters was a New Jersey tough guy who grew up in the shadow of New York City but went to college at, of all places, Western Illinois in obscure Macomb, Ill.

The three could not have come from more diverse areas, yet, for some reason, they hit it off immediately when all three converged on Green Bay in 1992. A bond formed then that was unbreakable for years but which has also been tested by extreme stress.

All three were essentially obscure, unknown players to most Packers fans. Favre was the hotshot quarterback that general manager Ron Wolf had given up a first-round draft pick to Atlanta for in a trade. Chmura was a rookie tight end taken in the sixth round of the draft that year and who had maybe a 50-50 chance of making the roster. Winters was already a six-year veteran when he came to the Packers from the old "Plan B" system that predated the current free agency. Winters was a long-snapper and versatile offensive lineman who had already played for the Cleveland Browns and Kansas City Chiefs.

Almost immediately, the three players gravitated toward each other, and none really understood why.

"I think it might have something to do with the fact that all three of us were fighting for jobs," Favre said. "We knew nothing was guaranteed, and we sort of looked to each other for support."

There was probably a lot of truth in Favre's words. Indeed, none of the three were anything special in 1992. Favre was unknown. Chmura had no credentials and Winters was already a journeyman who was probably already on the downside of his career.

Nonetheless, they became fast friends in training camp, and when it became clear that all three would have a vital role with the Packers, their friendship took deep root.

Soon the three were doing everything together. On their off days during the season, they'd play golf together when the weather allowed it. On their bye weeks, they'd travel to each other's homes. In the off season they'd take vacations together.

Chmura still recalls the day he went to Favre's home and watched in amazement and a little bit of horror as alligators wandered around 50 feet from the back door.

They would act like kids together, these high-paid and finely tuned athletes. They'd play practical jokes on each other and on unsuspecting teammates. If one was doing an interview with the media, more often than not one or both of the other two would show up to interrupt with hand and face gestures or a well-timed breaking of wind.

They were frat boys on spring break, and they had the times of their lives together. Soon their exploits made them fan favorites, and, as is usually the case when it involves the Packers, T-shirts appeared expounding on the wonders of the "Three Amigos," a nickname the three players did nothing to discourage.

They could be almost found anywhere and they'd always be together. Consider the postgame celebration after Super Bowl XXXI when Favre, Winters and Chmura cruised down Bourbon Street basking in the glory and celebrating as real friends who had reached a common goal.

But as much fun as they had away from the game, when they were on the field, they did their jobs superbly.

Favre grew rapidly and notoriously as the Packers' quarterback. Winters subbed for injured center James Campen that first year and went on to play every offensive line position at one point. Chmura battled injuries early but eventually became the NFL's prototype tight end.

As the Packers grew in power and prestige, the roles of all three evolved as well. Winters moved into the center spot and kept it for nearly nine full seasons. He was the captain of the offensive line, the guy who called the signals for everyone else on the line. He knew Favre's cadence and snap count almost better than the quarterback himself.

If a defensive lineman jumped offsides, Winters always knew to snap the ball ahead of time to get the penalty called. He would also constantly berate and antagonize opposing defenses and referees, often leaving Favre in stitches as he tried to call plays.

Winters also developed a reputation as one of the NFL's more, well, enthusiastic players. Some opposing defenses said he was flat-out dirty, but Winters, in his droll New York way, would simply say he was just playing the game the way it was meant to be played.

He became one of the NFL's most versatile offensive linemen even though he rarely received any accolades outside of Green Bay. But the Packers have always known how important he was.

Finally in 2002, at age 39, Winters lost his starting job at center to the younger Mike Flanagan. But instead of pouting, Winters accepted his role as a backup knowing that, the NFL being as it is, he'd probably get his chance to play again.

Sure enough, injuries decimated the Packers' front line, and Flanagan was forced to move to left tackle. Winters slipped seamlessly back to center as though he'd never left.

He still has no plans to retire, even though most players his age have long since retired and moved on to coaching careers. Winters will stay around as long as he feels he can play and, more important, as long as the Packers want him, because he can still be plugged into any position at a moment's notice and give a solid performance. Those players are rare.

Chmura had hoped to be that kind of player, too.

He came to the Packers as a 6'5", 250-pounder who could get downfield, make big catches and block. He was the perfect tight end for Mike Holmgren's West Coast offense.

But he struggled initially, first with injuries and later that rookie year with his inability to latch onto Holmgren's system. In fact, Chmura occupied a special place in Holmgren's always expanding doghouse because of his inability to learn the complicated system.

Chmura, known as "Chewy" to his teammates, would spend nights using Winters and Favre as his sounding boards, bouncing his frustrations and anger off his two best friends.

Then a funny thing happened. Eventually, it all began to make sense to Chmura. By 1995, he was becoming one of the league's top tight ends. He caught 54 passes for seven touchdowns and was named to his first Pro Bowl.

Of course, that renaissance may have a had a little something to do with the fact that the Packers traded for a former Pro Bowl tight end Keith Jackson, who would give the Packers a devastating 1-2 combination from the tight end spot. Jackson, who was playing with Miami at the time, initially said he'd go to Green Bay as soon as hell froze over—which is exactly the image he had of Northeastern Wisconsin. But eventually he relented after a long talk with former teammate Reggie White and joined the Packers.

Still, Chmura saw the handwriting on the wall, and he knew he had to produce, or Jackson would be allowed to show what he could do.

Over the next three seasons, he continued to be a solid contributor even though he was never able to fully put the injury bug behind him. Still, for a stretch from 1995-98, Favre and Chmura became one of deadliest tandems in the NFL, especially when the Packers found themselves near the goal line. It became common knowledge, even among Packers fans who only casually watched the game, that when the Packers found themselves inside the opponent's five-yard line, Favre would roll right and wait for Chmura to find a seam in the defense, where he'd hit him for another touchdown.

It wasn't rocket science, but it was well-conceived, well-executed football played by two guys who knew each other's thoughts almost too well.

But what had the makings of a great career never fully materialized for Chmura because of injuries that ranged from a bad shoulder to an injured knee to a strange foot injury in 1996. In fact, his career was put in jeopardy early in the 1999 season when he injured his neck against Detroit and missed the final 14 weeks of the season.

During his years in Green Bay, though, Chmura became one of the most visible and active players in the Green Bay community. He was well known for his charitable work and his tireless campaigning for Republican candidates in local, state and national offices. He was so popular in the community that he planned to incorporate his nickname and start a line of men's and women's swimwear known as "Chewy 89" (his jersey number).

Unfortunately for Chmura, those plans, and his NFL future, were derailed on an April night in 2000 when he let his celebrity get the better of him.

Chmura made an appearance at a high school graduation party for the daughter of a friend of his in the community where they lived north of Milwaukee. Eventually, it was alleged that Chmura spent time in a hot tub with two teenage girls and then allegedly had sex with a 17-year-old girl on the bathroom floor of the neighbor's house.

The alleged victim called police, and Chmura was arrested that night and eventually charged with third-degree sexual assault and child enticement. If found guilty on both counts, Chmura, the onetime Packers hero and role model, could spend 40 years in prison.

In a highly publicized and emotionally charged trial held nearly a year later, Chmura's personal life was laid bare for all to see, and if he wasn't guilty of a felony, many Wisconsin natives and even people around the nation at least looked on him as a scumball. He also looked to many like a raging hypocrite after his adamant criticism of

Center Frank Winters (left) and tight end Mark Chmura made up two-thirds of the famed "Three Amigos" that also included quarterback Brett Favre. *Photo courtesy of Vernon J. Biever*

President Clinton during his impeachment trial that stemmed from his liaison with a White House intern.

In the end, though, the evidence simply didn't support the girl's charges, and the jury needed just three hours, one of which they used for a lunch break, to find Chmura not guilty on both charges.

In a tearful press conference later that day, Chmura apologized to his wife, his kids and to all Packers fans, a large group of which attended the press conference wearing Chmura's No. 89 jersey.

Despite the verdict, the Packers knew they couldn't keep Chmura around. The neck injury that had forced him out the previous season had healed and he was given the go-ahead to play again. But he was damaged goods in Green Bay and he was released.

Chmura said he had held no grudges against the Packers but knew he could still play football for somebody. After his agent fielded several offers, including one from his hometown New England Patriots, he shocked many by announcing his retirement and his desire to study law, sparked by his trial.

He began clerking for the attorney who had defended him, Milwaukee's well-known Gerald Boyle, and he's now in the process of earning a law degree.

No one really knows how the trial affected the friendship between Favre and Chmura. Winters became a vehement defender of his friend during the trial and even dressed down a local reporter who wrote a column skewering Chmura.

Favre never made any public comments in defense of his buddy, and it struck many as strange, especially since those two were so tight for so long. But given a chance to comment on Chmura's legal woes several times, Favre always begged off and said justice had to run its course.

Today, Favre still won't talk about what happened with Chmura or whether those two remain friends or not. If that incident indeed splintered the friendship, it ended what was one of the great stories in Packers history.

Replacing a Legend

The Green Bay Packers are as much a state of mind as they are a collection of football players. Every Packer who's spent any time with the organization knows it's different from anyplace else in the NFL.

There is daunting history everywhere you look and with everything you see, and every player, whether they necessarily deserve it or not, finds his way into the pantheon of ex-Packers. That's just the way it is.

So to play for the Packers is to inherit a legacy. Each new player carries the torch for the player who came before, whether they look at it that way or not.

It's difficult enough to step into that situation when you're the new guy having to replace someone who couldn't quite cut the mustard. Imagine having to try to fill the role of a player who, to many even today, still symbolizes what is good and true and right about the Green Bay Packers.

After all, it took the Packers 20 years to find a worthy successor to Bart Starr, and no young quarterback anywhere wants to be the one who has to step in when Brett Favre decides to retire. The pressure, the expectations, the demands will be crushing and there will be an extremely small window of opportunity for that player to prove he can do the job as well.

That was the situation that faced Jim Carter in 1972. A former University of Minnesota fullback, Carter was drafted in 1970 and moved to outside linebacker. At this stage, the Packers were still living somewhat off their remarkable run in the 1960s, and the legend of the Packers still pulsed.

But things were changing. The stars of the 1960s were getting older and starting to retire or move on to other teams. The plays they used to make with ease three years earlier suddenly became more difficult. Vince Lombardi was gone, and Phil Bengston was finding out for himself how difficult it was to replace a legend.

The world was evolving, and the 1960s Packers, as good as they were, were already becoming relics in their own museum.

So new blood began flowing through the roster, and one of those players was Carter, who would go on to learn all too painfully that taking over a position doesn't necessarily mean taking over the fans who came with it.

In 1971, it was Carter's turn to replace a legend. He beat out beloved Ray Nitschke in training camp and took over as starting linebacker, the spot Nitschke had patrolled with a controlled fury since 1958. With his bald head and craggy face, he was the perfect image of the NFL linebacker and he had run the defense for years, to the point where many fans couldn't imagine the Packers without Nitschke in the middle.

On top of that, he adored the Packers and proved to be one of the great ambassadors for the city and the franchise. He would play forever if given the chance.

But his days as a quality linebacker were dwindling and he knew it. All he had ever asked, though, was that he be given a chance to lose the job fair and square—as any old warrior would. If some young pup came along who was better than he was, so be it.

That didn't happen in this case—at least Nitschke didn't think so.

Instead, coach Dan Devine gave the job to Carter, enraging Nitschke.

What made matters worse was that Carter failed to show the proper deference to a player who had done so much for the organization, who would be a Hall of Famer one day, and who was such an unabashed fan of the Packers' mystique. Carter simply thought he was a better player and deserved the starting nod over the aging Nitschke.

But fans didn't see it that way. The didn't like the new guy's attitude, and they especially didn't like that he not only replaced Nitschke but derided him on top of it. As a result, that made Carter's career in Green Bay something less than the storybook so many other ex-Packers experienced.

"I was never accepted," Carter said once when talking about his Packers days that, in truth, were a lot more successful that many people realize. He was a Pro Bowler, the leading tackler, a solid linebacker who made the plays he had to for a succession of Packers teams that simply weren't very good.

Of course, it didn't help matters that, after Nitschke retired in 1972, he continued to live in the area and could be found, more often that not, at local restaurants, bars and stores talking about the Packers and the sad state to which they had fallen. For Packers fans, Nitschke was the constant memory of the golden, glorious past when the Packers were titans striding the earth.

Carter was the dismal present and depressing future. He was the symbol of everything wrong with the Packers, the new breed of players who made a mockery of the legend. He was booed mercilessly by the hometown folks and rarely, if ever, saw the side of being a Green Bay Packer that made it so special for so many other players. He could have been a fan favorite like Nitschke, especially with his glib manner, but it never happened, and it bothers him even today.

In later years, especially after he retired in 1978, Carter admitted he could have handled the situation in Green Bay better. He knew he should have kept his mouth shut and not criticized an icon like Nitschke. He knew he should have played the game the best he could and not worried about what people thought of him.

But he also wishes fans would have given him a chance. It wasn't his fault, after all, that he had to replace Nitschke—in time someone was going to anyway.

Carter went on to become a successful businessman in Eau Claire, regretting what had transpired in Green Bay and wishing, on some level, it had never happened.

Nitschke maintained his role as the goodwill ambassador for the Green Bay Packers. He agonized more than anyone when the Packers went into their 20-year funk, but he was always there to say things would get better, even if deep down he wasn't sure they ever would.

And no one was happier when the Packers returned to prominence in the 1990s. One of the enduring images is of Nitschke standing in the team's media auditorium

Hall of Fame linebacker Ray Nitschke embodied everything that the Packers were in the 1960s, and even after he retired, the Packers were his life. *Photo courtesy of Vernon J. Biever*

during a press conference prior to Super Bowl XXXI, his face enveloped by a huge smile.

"Isn't this great?" he said to anyone who wanted to listen.

His life had come full circle. He joined the Packers when they were on the cusp of greatness in the 1950s and he had seen his beloved team come back into prominence. And he was truly happy.

But that didn't cushion the blow for Packers fans when they learned on March 8, 1998 that Nitschke had died unexpectedly of a heart attack at the age of 61.

He was a three-time All-Pro, played in 190 games as a Packer (the second most in club history) and he was named a member of the NFL's 50th anniversary and 75th anniversary teams. More important, he embodied everything the Packers were and could be. He loved the Packers perhaps more than any player the franchise has ever known, and the team's success was inextricably tied to his happiness. He is missed by Packers fans even today.

Jim Carter would have liked to have known just a little of what that felt like.

Butler Did It

He stood on the Packers' practice field, oblivious to an approaching summer storm, and talked about what he wanted to bring the Green Bay Packers one day.

He was just another rookie, though he was a second-round draft pick of whom great things were expected. Still, as he stood on the practice field after another training camp practice, he said all the same stuff that every rookie said.

"I want to help the team. I'll just do what they ask me to do. This is a great honor."

It all sounded the same, as though it came from the rookies' handbook titled, "What to Tell the Media Before it Becomes Obvious We Can't Really Play."

It seems easy to say now, but LeRoy Butler really did know what he was talking about. And while he was a reticent rookie in 1990, getting Butler to open up after that was no trick at all.

It is rare in these days of free agency for one player to stick with the same team for an entire career. But LeRoy Butler did, even though he had more than a few opportunities over the years to go elsewhere. He was a Packer, and somewhere along the line, he grew to understand that in a way few players do. And after his reluctant retirement prior to the 2002 season, he will take his place among the most popular, productive and successful players this franchise has ever known.

He would go on to redefine the position of free safety in the NFL thanks to a scheme worked out with his favorite defensive coordinator, Fritz Shurmur. Under Shurmur, Butler would make safety an activist position where he would force the play instead of waiting for the play to come to him. He would blitz and he would drop back in coverage. He would come up to play the run and, on occasion, he'd smack a tight end on the line of scrimmage.

He wasn't the biggest guy to the play the position at 5'11" and about 200 pounds, and he wasn't a particularly big hitter. But over time, Butler developed into one of the best safeties in the game, and, not coincidentally, his rapid improvement mirrored the improvement in the Packers in the 1990s.

But it didn't start out that way. Taken by the Packers in the second round of the 1990 draft, Butler came out of Florida State as the other cornerback across from Deion Sanders. But Butler could play the game in his own right and, in truth, was able to flourish in college because of all the attention directed at Sanders.

But when he came to Green Bay, the Packers weren't exactly sure what to do with him. Defensive coordinator Hank Bullough saw a kid with great athletic skills but wasn't sure if he was a cornerback or a safety. So they kept him at cornerback for two seasons before he was shifted, for good, to safety in 1992.

But it was long before that when Butler proved he was more than a good player—he was also a media darling. Quotable, affable, intelligent and more than occasionally outrageous, the local media hung on his every word even if sometimes Butler himself wasn't sure what he was going to say. He eventually developed a routine in the Packers' locker room, where, every Thursday, he would meet at noon in front of his locker prior to practice and hold court with all the media.

It was then and there that he'd tell the people holding the cameras, tape recorders, notebooks and microphones his views on everything from that week's opponent to what he was getting for Christmas to his views on world politics.

He was never reluctant to tell anyone what he thought about anything, especially when his act went national and his viewpoints could be heard not just in Green Bay but around the country. Sometimes, that wasn't necessarily a good thing.

One of his more legendary pronouncements came in training camp prior to the 1997 season. The Packers had just come off winning Super Bowl XXXI, and they looked every bit as strong going into that season. Indeed, the team looked so strong that Butler took the opportunity to say that the Packers could very well go 19-0 that season. The statement wasted no time going national.

For coach Mike Holmgren, it was the worst thing Butler could have possibly said. Not only did it give the appearance that the Packers were arrogant (which they probably were, let's face it), but it gave every team they'd play that season another reason to go after the defending Super Bowl champs. Holmgren, a coach who wanted control of every aspect of the football operation, called Butler into his office and told him how unhappy he was with his safety's bravado. But Holmgren had also learned long ago that the only person who can silence Butler is Butler.

In the second game of that season, the Packers went to Philadelphia and played horrendously. Still, trailing 10-9, the Packers had a chance to win the game when they drove deep into Eagles territory in the final seconds.

Then, as the Packers lined up for the game-winning field goal, a torrential downpour lasting maybe two minutes hit Veterans Stadium. It wasn't much, but it was just enough to cause rookie kicker Ryan Longwell to slip and miss a 29-yard field goal.

"So much for going 19-0," Holmgren cracked without humor after the game.

Butler realized that even he might have stepped over the line with that prediction, and when a reporter asked him a week later about a prediction for another game, he said simply, "Don't ask me. I'm the stupid SOB who said we'd go 19-0."

Perhaps his comments wouldn't have drawn as much attention if he were a backup safety. But the fact was, here was one of the premier players in the league who loved to talk to the media even when there were times he probably shouldn't have.

He long ago spoke of his dislike for the Minnesota Vikings and what he saw as the pretentious attitude of star wide receiver Cris Carter. A born-again Christian, Butler was skeptical of just how devout Carter really was and offered examples of how Carter would resort to dirty play, especially in a pile-up.

Butler would sometimes criticize his own teammates who he thought weren't playing as well as they should. He would criticize himself for not giving the effort he should have. But he always had something to say.

At least he did until the 1999 season under Ray Rhodes, when it was obvious there was something wrong with the Packers and in the locker room.

For six weeks, he stopped talking to the media and when asked why, his answer was simply, "I don't have anything to say." That's when many people realized that if Butler didn't have anything to say, there must be plenty to say.

Eventually he ended his media blackout, but it was obvious he still wasn't happy with what was happening on or off the field. He spoke of fractures within the team and of how the Packers of the years before were changing—and not necessarily for the better.

His role was changing too. Under Shurmur, he had become one of the NFL's top safeties. But under new defensive coordinator Emmitt Thomas, Butler was pulled back off the line of scrimmage and told to assume a more traditional safety role. The previous three seasons, Butler accumulated 13 1/2 quarterbacks sacks, but in 1999 he had just one, and he was frustrated. He even called Holmgren and Shurmur, who had moved with the head coach to the Seattle Seahawks, to vent his frustration.

But Butler did his job, was credited with 67 tackles and two interceptions, and fully expected Rhodes back the next year. Maybe that's why he was one of the most surprised players when he was called late in the night after the final game of the season and told that Rhodes, along with his entire staff, had been fired.

All through that crazy night and into the early morning, Butler fielded phone calls from flabbergasted teammates asking him if he knew what was happening. And Butler wasn't exactly in peak form since he was suffering from a painful shoulder injury suffered in that last game.

He may have been shocked, but he wasn't especially disappointed Rhodes was gone. His replacement, Mike Sherman, brought in a new, young defensive coordinator in Ed Donatell, who made it clear he would allow Butler to do what he did best.

But no one would do for Butler what Fritz Shurmur did. Hired in 1994 to replace Rhodes, who left to become defensive coordinator in San Francisco, Shurmur was wonderfully, irreverently old-school. His was a defense predicated on attack, attack, attack, which had worked for him through 30 years of coaching in places as varied as Albion College in Michigan to the Los Angeles Rams.

Butler and Shurmur hit it off immediately and, under the old coach's guidance, Butler flourished.

In 1996, Butler had perhaps the best season an NFL safety could likely have. Unleashed to play on defense the way he felt he needed to play, Butler posted 92 tackles, intercepted five passes and had 13 passes defensed. More amazing were his 6 1/2 sacks in which he'd delay at the line of scrimmage and then swoop in on the quarterback, usually from the blind side. It was a devastating and relatively new concept, and it gave the Packers one more pass rusher to go along with ends Reggie White and Sean Jones. It was a major reason why the Packers won the Super Bowl and had the top-rated defense in the league.

"I've never had more fun playing," he said.

Two years later, Shurmur was gone as he joined Holmgren in Seattle. But it got even worse when it was revealed that Shurmur was suffering from cancer. Before he even coached a game in Seattle, he returned to his home in Suamico, Wis. where he had decided to settle and live out his days. In the summer of 1999, Shurmur died and Butler was crushed. At the funeral, Butler was one of the pallbearers.

Through his career, Butler had chances to leave the Packers. He knew he could probably make more money someplace, and the Jacksonville, Fla. native, who still lived there in the off season, could escape the punishing Green Bay winters. But he never seriously considered other offers.

He was annoyed at the Packers on more than one occasion, though, especially when then general manager Ron Wolf said Butler had been out of shape heading into the 1997 season. The public recrimination embarrassed Butler and caused him briefly to think about going somewhere else.

But in the end, he knew he was a Packer and he wanted to stay a Packer. Indeed, he took the role so seriously that he had his contract reworked several times in the final few years to help the Packers with their salary cap and allow them to sign free agents they otherwise couldn't have gone after.

He likely would have also become the longest tenured Packer in team history, surpassing Bart Starr, if not for the brutal circumstances that are football.

In a November 18, 2001 game against the Atlanta Falcons, Butler made the kind of tackle he's made a thousands times before. But this time, he fractured his shoulder blade, a painful and unusual injury that ended his season. It was expected he could return the following season, but it was also becoming clear that he was not the same player he'd been. Sure, the instincts and experience were there, but it took a half-second longer to get where he needed to be. And never the fastest player around even in his prime, he was clearly starting to slow down even more.

As the Packers looked at 2002, they knew they had to start grooming a replacement for Butler, and it seemed to fall on Antuan Edwards, an underachieving former first-round draft pick. The plan was to work Edwards into the starting lineup and have Butler on hand as his mentor and backup.

Butler seemed OK with the idea as well until the medical reports came back and offered a different scenario. The shoulder blade hadn't healed properly, and for Butler to subject it to more punishment would be foolish and possibly life-altering. Faced with no other real alternative, Butler announced his retirement on July 18, 2002, just as training camp was starting.

It was a surprisingly unemotional affair, especially for a gregarious player like Butler who had played 12 seasons and 181 games with the same team. But maybe he understood better than many players in his situation that the time had come and he was leaving, more or less, on his terms.

"Just knowing I can retire today, that all my football cards are in that green and white jersey, I mean, that's priceless," Butler said at his final press conference. "People say, 'How can you give away a million dollars last year [in a contract restructuring]?' Easy, easy because I want to stay here."

The Game of the Name

Do anything of any significance as a member of this football team and chances are you'll get something named after you. A street, a school, a shopping center, it doesn't really matter. Heck, in the mid-1990s, when Brett Favre was weaving his magic with the Packers, hospitals in the state noticed a huge increase in newborns being named "Brett."

They are everywhere in Green Bay. From a neighborhood in town where the street names all honor former Packers stars to perhaps the most famous name of all, Lombardi Avenue, which runs north and south in front of, right, Lambeau Field.

Across the street from the stadium is Holmgren Way, which has a side street called Brett Favre Pass. It runs right past the Ray Nitschke practice field which is just down the road from the Don Hutson Center and is right next to the Clark Hinkle practice field.

There are some notable omissions, of course. There is nothing, at least not yet, for general manager Ron Wolf, who helped turn the Packers from a mediocre, directionless franchise in 1991 to an eventual Super Bowl champ. Wolf has always said he doesn't want anything named for him, but chances are he will be ignored. He simply meant too much for too long to this franchise.

There has also been nothing in honor of quarterback/coach Bart Starr, one of the quintessential representatives that the organization has ever known. Not that plans haven't been floated before, but sometimes it's just not so easy renaming a road, even if it is for someone as noteworthy as Starr.

For example, after a new arena was built across the street from Lambeau Field, the namesake of the arena, Dick Resch, who owns KI Industries in Green Bay, approached local leaders about the possibility of renaming Packer Drive (what else?), a small road in front of the new arena that connects Oneida Street and Holmgren Way (we'll get to that one in a minute) to Bart Starr Drive.

Seems simple enough. But, of course, it wasn't.

First, local officials were concerned that $500,000 expected from Resch and his partners for an honorary Starr plaza (complete with a statue) hadn't been received yet. And that would certainly go a longway toward a renaming project.

But there were more problems, especially when it became clear from local businesses that renaming another street would cause all sorts of advertising and mail problems.

Others, however, feel it's appropriate to honor one of the great players, and great gentlemen, that the franchise has known. A board meeting is scheduled down the road to decide if the project will go ahead or not. Stay tuned.

The most controversial renaming involved Holmgren, who, like all the others who have had streets named for them, felt a little uneasy about it. Nonetheless, in a wave of emotion after winning Super Bowl XXXI, officials in Brown County and Ashwaubenon, where, technically, the Packers play, decided it was time to honor the coach who made it all happen.

For years it was called Gross Avenue, and it stretched from Lombardi Avenue east. It was nothing special, really. It was just a road with businesses, a restaurant or two and a couple of bars. It was like a million other roads in a million other places.

But the powers that be decided it was perfect to rename Holmgren Way. And while businesspeople along the road thought it was a fine idea in theory, in practice it would prove to be a serious pain in the neck.

That's because every business would have to go about changing the address on every piece of letterhead, every advertisement, everything that set their business apart from others. And while the cost itself was minimal, it was an inconvenience.

There was also the little matter of when the decision was finalized to rename the road, the rumors were already swirling that Holmgren might be leaving for greener pastures. Did anyone really want to name a road for a coach who was thinking of leaving?

The answer, apparently, was yes. So in the summer of 1998, a grand ceremony was held and Gross Avenue was officially renamed Holmgren Way. The coach and his family were more than a little sheepish during the event, but they also knew that it was indeed a big deal and they knew that it took a fairly special accomplishment to disrupt the status quo like that.

The concerns of the doubters, though, proved accurate as less than a year later, as the rumors grew stronger and eventually into fact, Holmgren departed to become general manager and head coach of the Seahawks. Some locals were outraged that they had spent the time and money to rename a road for somebody who left.

Eventually cooler heads prevailed, and community leaders decided it would be even more expensive and troublesome to turn the name back to what it was. Besides, there was no denying what Holmgren did for the team despite his leaving. And today, Holmgren Way is slowly but surely becoming a part of the everyday lexicon of Green Bay travelers.

A Sad Life

No one knew of the demons that haunted Lionel Aldridge for so many years. To many—to most, actually—he was just the big, burly soft-spoken defensive right end who was a key member of the Packers' NFL dominance in the early to mid-1960s.

He was a fourth-round draft pick in 1963 out of Utah State, and he slipped right into a starting defense that was the best in the NFL and included future Hall of Famers like Willie Davis, Ray Nitschke, Henry Jordan, Herb Adderly and Willie Wood.

And while Aldridge always went about his job quietly and efficiently until his retirement in 1971, no one knew the pain that was brewing just below the surface and how, in later years, it would develop into a full-fledged phobia.

For years, Aldridge battled paranoia and schizophrenia that would eventually force him to lose everything before he was able to bounce back and tell his story of survival to others who needed help, too.

Aldridge, a member of the Packers Hall of Fame, wasn't really sure where his descent in mental illness really began, but he does know that it nearly ruined his life. He would recount frightening incidents when he'd black out and have no idea where he was or how he got there.

He talked of the day he was driving from Milwaukee to Madison for a lunch appointment, blacked out and found himself in Rhinelander, in far north Wisconsin, at 4 a.m. the next morning.

"I had no idea how I got there," he said.

He talked of the hallucinations that taunted him endlessly. He talked of a plate of spaghetti that turned into worms and how trees would talk to him and how people would emerge from the cracks in the road.

And, scariest of all, he talked of his constant desire, his need almost, to kill himself. In one remarkable talk in Appleton, Wis. one night, he told the audience he was especially proud of himself that night.

"I had assumed I wasn't going to make it here tonight because I was going to kill myself," he said simply. "I knew exactly how I was going to do it. All day long I've been having thoughts of suicide and I didn't want to die."

The fact that Aldridge made the trip and delivered the talk was the highlight of his day.

"I could just hug myself for surviving today," he said.

At one time, his mental illness forced him into homelessness and divorce and estrangement from his family. But in the late '90s, he found medication that kept the demons at bay and allowed him to be a powerful and passionate advocate for mental illness.

Unfortunately, this story doesn't have a happy ending. Even though he had found a certain peace in his life and was moving toward reconciliation with his kids, Aldridge was found dead in February, 1998 in his Milwaukee apartment of an apparent heart attack. He was just 57.

His goal of reshaping his life and living the way he wanted was cut short, though his message remains.

"Nobody wants to be like this," he said. "And everyone has to know there is help."

Other Quarterbacks

His name is Kyle Wachholz, and he played exactly zero snaps for the Green Bay Packers. Yet in his three-year "career" he managed to stick around to be part of some of the best teams in Packers history.

His was an odd story that shows just how important it is to be in the right place at the right time even if you can't do anything especially well.

Waccholz was a seventh-round draft pick of the Packers in 1996, a quarterback from Southern California who wasn't even a starter for his college team. But he had those qualities that coach Mike Holmgren liked. He was tall, he was rangy and he had a pretty good arm. Of course, he had no shot at playing with the Packers since they already had a fair quarterback in place already.

But who knew? Maybe in time he could develop into something, and if there was one thing Holmgren was especially good at, it was developing quarterbacks.

That was before, however, the Packers got him into mini-camps and found out that while the big guy had decent physical skills, he was a little lacking in the mental part of the game.

He was a nice kid, a kind of surfer dude who came from the beaches of Southern California and never really had to think too much about anything. He was engaging and unassuming and thoroughly nonplussed about his surroundings and what was expected of him.

But he clearly struggled to get a grip on the Packers' complex offense—though he certainly wasn't the only one to have been perplexed by it over the years.

Still there was the feeling that Waccholz wasn't exactly the sharpest tool in the shed.

One local radio reporter approached the subject one day in training camp.

"You've got this reputation of not being the most cerebral quarterback around," he asked. "Do you want to refute that?"

Waccholz looked at the reporter blankly and said, "Sure, if you tell me what cerebral means."

He was placed on the Packers' practice squad that year, meaning he couldn't compete in any games unless he cleared waivers. But there was no chance of him playing that year or, as it turned out, any other year.

He stayed on the practice squad as the Packers won the Super Bowl and he was there again in 1998 when the Packers went back to the Super Bowl. Still he had not taken a snap either in a preseason or regular-season game.

The next year, the Packers tried an experiment and put Waccholz at tight end when it became clear he wasn't going to cut it at quarterback. But he was injured in training camp and eventually cut.

Officially, he was never on the Packers' roster, but he still traveled to two Super Bowls, was with the Packers nearly three seasons and never took a single snap.

There have been other quarterbacks who flashed briefly across the landscape before disappearing.

One who made a brief appearance and managed to latch on somewhere else was a fellow named Kurt Warner.

After a record-setting career at Northern Iowa, Warner was ignored by every team in the 1994 draft. But the Packers signed him as a free agent mostly to give a break to the other quarterbacks, who were an All-Star lineup at the time including Favre, Mark Brunell and Ty Detmer.

It was clear that Warner had no future with the Packers, but as with many players who come into training camp, they hope their performance in backup roles will catch the eye of other teams who can use them.

"I can learn a lot from these guys," Warner said at the time, though he never quite took advantage of the opportunity.

He stayed pretty much to himself, especially since Favre, Brunell and Detmer had developed a close relationship. Years later, when asked his memories of Warner, Favre shrugged and said he couldn't remember much except for a passing drill when Warner was called on to take part but declined because he didn't know the plays well enough.

That showed the Packers all they needed to see, and he was cut midway through camp.

Warner, of course, has since gone on to his own glory. After he was cut by Green Bay, he went back to Iowa and worked as stock clerk before latching on to the Arena Football League. Eventually he signed with the St. Louis

Rams as a backup to Trent Green, and, well, the rest is the stuff of legend.

The uncertain kid had blossomed into a confident quarterback, and he led the Rams to a Super Bowl title in 1999. A year later he was named the league MVP.

Maybe he learned something from his time with the Packers after all.

Kirk Baumgartner had the best arm anybody had seen in a long time. Sure he played at the Division III level, flinging passes around the neighborhood at the nearby University of Wisconsin-Stevens Point.

But a good arm is a good arm, and the fact that Baumgartner set a Division III record for passing was at least worthy enough for the Packers to expend a seventh-round draft pick in 1990 to look at.

It had the makings for one of those great success stories, too. Small-town boy from a small college makes good with his favorite team. It had everything.

Except, that is, a happy ending. As Baumgartner and the Packers found out together, college football isn't the NFL, and completing passes against Division III secondaries is only slightly easier than trying to complete them against NFL players.

And then there was the playbook. Coach Lindy Infante was like every other coach in the NFL in that his offensive playbook was the size of the Guttenberg Bible. There were checkdowns and checkoffs and audibles and hot reads and route adjustments and so much else to learn that Baumgartner's head would have exploded if it wasn't stuck inside a helmet.

Unfortunately, for many quarterbacks who try to play at the pro level, the shock hits quickly that you're not as good and not as smart as you once thought. The plays that came so easily in high school and college were impossible to make at this level, and Baumgartner learned it rapidly.

Infante tried to put the best face on it he could, but he admitted that his rookie quarterback just wasn't getting it. Infante wanted to keep him around long enough to at least see what he could do under fire, but his inability to grasp even the most basic aspects of the offense made it impossible.

Baumgartner, the great experiment and the proof that Division III guys could play after all, barely lasted to the first cutdown when he was mercifully released.

Baumgartner seemed to read the writing on the wall, too, and decided a career in football wasn't for him, so he went into business back in Stevens Point.

Robbie Bosco is still viewed today as one of the greatest blunders the Packers ever made on draft day—and they've made some beauties—and a testament to the sometimes pig-headedness of the franchise.

In fairness to the Packers, Bosco, a third-round selection in 1986 out of Brigham Young, was viewed as a can't-miss pro prospect after his wonderful college career in which he piled up more passing yards than any Cougar quarterback except Steve Young and Jim McMahon. And the Packers, always on the lookout for a quarterback, saw Bosco as the answer to their prayers.

There was just one small problem. While Bosco was tearing up college football, he was also tearing up his throwing shoulder. He knew as a college senior there was a problem but dismissed it as overuse—after all, he threw 511 passes that year.

If the Packers knew he had an arm problem, they didn't think it was serious enough to bypass him in the draft, and they giddily and quickly took him in the third round and all but handed him the starting job the following year.

But Bosco had a rotator cuff injury that, in the days before all the remarkable surgical techniques that are available today, was basically a career ender.

The injury plagued Bosco all through his first training camp with the Packers, and it was then that even coach Forrest Gregg decided his new quarterback needed surgery. The renowned orthopedic surgeon, Dr. Frank Jobe, did the surgery and said Bosco had a 50-50 chance of playing again.

He missed all of the 1987 season in rehab but felt he could come back in 1988. But during the rigors of training camp that year, Bosco's arm never came around and, after three years and no appearances in any games, the Packers gave up on him.

Tackling the Problem

In the mindset of general manager Ron Wolf, you could never be too rich, too smart or have too many offensive linemen. Maybe that's why he always placed such a high premium on them during the draft. In fact, in the nine years he had a direct hand in running the Packers' drafts, he took an offensive lineman with the No. 1 pick three times—guard Aaron Taylor in 1994, tackle John Michels in 1996 and tackle Ross Verba in 1997.

Both Michels and Verba were left tackles, easily the most important position on the offensive line because that was the player who protected the quarterback's blind spot against the defense's top pass rusher.

For years, left tackle had been in the capable if uninspiring hands of Ken Ruettgers, who had become known more for his penchant for holding out of training camp than what he did on the field.

But he was competent and solid and was one of those players the coaches could stick out there and usually forget about.

But Ruettgers was coming to the end of his career in the mid-1990s, and with Brett Favre only now blossoming in his career, the Packers needed to look at a new left tackle.

For reasons still surpassing understanding, Wolf wanted Michels, a converted defensive end at Southern Cal who had played tackle for just one season in college. But Wolf loved his size (six foot six, 300 pounds), and he was convinced that his best football was still ahead of him.

The plan was for Michels to learn at the knee of the wily veteran Ruettgers and then take over when Ruettgers was ready to call it quits.

But the best-laid plans don't always work out, and of course, they didn't in this case. A succession of injuries over the years had worn down Ruettgers, and at the beginning of the 1996 training camp, due mostly to a knee injury, he was simply unable to play.

That thrust Michels squarely into the forefront at a time when he clearly wasn't ready. But the Packers really had no other choices at the moment, so they inserted the raw rookie and hoped he could at least hold off the raging tide of defensive players who would be coming after Favre. The first test was a relatively meaningless preseason home

Left tackle Ken Ruettgers labored for 12 years in the trenches for some truly awful teams. He finally had to retire midway through the 1996 season due to injuries and never enjoyed the fruits of that Super Bowl win. *Photo courtesy of Vernon J. Biever*

opener against New England, in which the coaches watched anxiously to see if Michels would hold up.

After the game, Michels, an affable and engaging kid who never quite understood what the fuss was all about, gave himself a passing grade. Favre, who played sparingly, said simply, "I was standing at the end, so I guess he did OK."

The experiment seemed like it might work. Michels appeared to have the physical skills to overcome his woeful inexperience, and for most of the season, he did OK. Meanwhile, Ruettgers, who was sitting out and hoping to heal up, realized by midseason it wasn't going to happen. After an aborted effort to play midway through the season, he announced his retirement.

But with the playoffs approaching and the Packers favored to win it all, OK was not good enough for coach Mike Holmgren. In a first-round playoff game against San Francisco, the Packers made a shocking decision and pulled Michels out of the starting lineup and replaced him with veteran Bruce Wilkerson.

"I needed to be sure at that position, and I just wasn't," Holmgren said. "This is the playoffs."

Of course it took him an entire season to figure that out, but once he made the move, he had no intention of looking back. Michels was hurt and angry and embarrassed, but there was little he could do about it.

Wilkerson took over at left tackle and played splendidly. He provided the experience and quality that Michels lacked, and he helped the Packers roll to a Super Bowl title.

Michels was never quite the same again. Bothered by a knee injury of his own, he furiously tried to rehab in the off season and win back the starting job he felt was taken away from him.

But the Packers had already moved on, and in a move that spoke volumes to Michels, Green Bay made Iowa tough guy Ross Verba their top pick in the next draft. By the end of that year, Michels was gone.

But Verba presented his own set of problems. He was confident to the point of arrogance, a far cry from the quieter and more respectful Michels. Verba maintained from the beginning that he cared not at all what people thought of him or how he approached his work. He was covered in tattoos, including a multicolored, almost floral pattern on his back. When asked what it signified, he smiled wryly and said, "It's personal and nobody would understand anyway."

He also wore his religious beliefs on his sleeve, though some teammates doubted his sincerity. He kept to himself, insisted he had no close friends on the team and did what he wanted when he wanted.

But he could play the game. That much everybody knew about him.

Still, he got off on the wrong foot with Holmgren and his teammates by holding out for most of training camp over a contract dispute. And there was nothing Holmgren hated worse than a player missing valuable training camp due to a contract spat.

Finally, Verba agreed to a deal late in August, but he had missed the kind of practice time that was nearly impossible to recover. He had also already damaged his reputation with his teammates because of his public comments about how the Packers were handling the negotiations.

After all, here was a team poised to win a second straight Super Bowl. They didn't need some young punk telling them what to do and how to do it. So in his first practice, Verba was pounded on unmercifully.

He received late hits and cheap shots all designed to let him know the rest of the team wasn't happy. Late in the day, Verba decided he'd had enough. After another late smack from defensive end Keith McKenzie, Verba started swinging. The two men went at it at just long enough and stopped before anyone got hurt.

The Packers had sent their message. But Verba had sent his, too. He wasn't going to be pushed around by anybody, and that was the attitude everyone wanted to see.

Despite Holmgren's annoyance with Verba's holdout, he also understood this guy was a street fighter who would protect Favre with his life if he had to. As a result, he slipped him into the starting lineup early that season.

And when asked how he thought he did his first game, he smiled.

"How do you think I did?" he said. "I give myself an A-plus."

Confidence was not an issue with Ross Verba, but he continued to have run-ins with Holmgren, who wanted the youngster to abide by his strict code. Verba had no intention of it.

He came to training camp one year with flowing curly locks down almost to his shoulders, once more igniting the fury of his coach.

Verba said the new look was just a lark, something to do in the off season to ease his boredom. But as soon as it became clear that Holmgren didn't like the look, Verba decided to keep it awhile. It was one more point of contention between the coach and the player who never did quite see eye to eye with each other the entire time they were together.

Of course, Verba eventually trimmed his hair, but only after he'd again made his point that nobody would tell him what he could or couldn't do.

After four years, unrestricted free agency came calling and Verba took a lucrative offer from Cleveland after it became obvious the Packers had no intention of trying to re-sign him.

G Whiz

If it's not the most famous emblem in American sports, it's certainly in the top two or three.

What's more recognizable than the white "G" on the side of the Packers' helmet? It's been there for more than 40 years, as constant as the sunrise and as recognizable as Santa Claus.

While other teams have gone through wholesale changes in their uniform designs, including team colors and insignias, the Packers have remained blissfully anachronistic. They know what works and they stick with it.

Sure, there was that little incident a few years ago when general manager Ron Wolf wanted to tinker with the team colors and logo, but after a public backlash, he backed off. And for as long as anybody can remember, the Packers' familiar G has been worn by Hall of Famers and rookies alike.

It has also been a symbol many teams around the country tried to duplicate.

Consider the University of Georgia and the black "G" on the side of its helmet that many people are convinced was copied by the Packers. In truth, it was the other way around.

In 1964, Georgia football coach Vince Dooley was looking to update his team's uniform and always liked the look of the Packers' classic helmet. In a wondrous piece of simplicity, Georgia athletic director Joel Eaves called Packers coach Vince Lombardi and team president Dom Olejniczak and asked if the school could use it too.

They were given permission, and Georgia has kept the look ever since. Ironically, other football teams—from Pop Warner to college—have also tried to use the symbol, but the Packers have cracked down, citing trademark infringement.

The Golden Boy

Perhaps no player in team history has relished his association with the team more than Paul Hornung.

Nearly 40 years later, Hornung still basks in the glow of his Packers years even though he had already made a reputation for himself as a Heisman Trophy winner at Notre Dame. His years with the Packers were marked with incredible highs and staggering lows, but through it all he never lost his zest for living or his love of the game—both on the field and off.

The stories of Hornung during his Packers days are legendary now, and he has done little over the years to disavow many of them. And while he thrived on his reputation as a scoundrel, playboy and rapscallion, no one could ever deny his often breathtaking ability on the field.

What many people may not remember is that the Packers originally wanted to make him a quarterback when he was taken in the 1957 draft. At that stage, the Packers were pathetic. Since their last NFL title in 1944, the Packers had managed just three winning records after that and none since 1947. Curly Lambeau, the Packers' founder, architect and great name to date had already seen the writing on the wall and bailed out as coach after the 1949 season, and the two coaches since then, Gene Ronzani and Lisle Blackbourn, had done nothing.

So Hornung was a breath of fresh air for a stagnant franchise even though in his first two seasons, the Packers remained horrible, winning just four games first under Blackbourn and then in one disastrous season with Ray "Scooter" McLean.

Then it all changed in 1959 when Vince Lombardi saw how badly Hornung was being utilized and moved him to halfback full-time where he belonged.

Hornung went on to lead the NFL in scoring the next three years and was the NFL MVP in 1960 and 1961. Hornung, like many of the Packers in that era, still speaks of Lombardi with a hushed reverence, and not only for the wins and success he brought them, but for the way he got the best out of each of them.

And it was obvious early just what kind of pull the Packers' head coach had as well, especially when it involved his best players.

It was a very different world in the early 1960s. Football wasn't a year-round requirement the way it is for players now. There were no mini-camps, and off-season training consisted of a player cutting back to one six-pack of beer a day. Many players, most players actually, had full-time jobs in the off season, because playing football didn't pay enough to cover the bills.

That's why so many ex-players even today still own car dealerships or restaurants or insurance agencies. It's what they started as players and what they've built since they left the game.

As well, many players were part of active military service back then. They were either in National Guard or in the reserves because it was the obligation of everyone to serve their time in the military. And sometimes world affairs overwhelmed professional sports.

One classic example came on December 31, 1961, when the Packers were preparing to meet the New York Giants for the NFL title. But over in Berlin, Germany, a showdown of potential, and literal, nuclear proportions was brewing between the United States and the Soviet Union, and the National Guard was being activated. That unit included three Packers, starters all—linebacker Ray Nitschke, wide receiver Boyd Dowler and Hornung.

Knowing their chances of beating the Giants were minuscule without those three, Lombardi actually called President John Kennedy, a burgeoning Packers fan himself, and asked for help. Kennedy called the commander of the unit, and all three players were allowed to play.

Hornung, with just one practice under his belt, still scored 19 points in the game on a touchdown run, three field goals and four extra points, and the Packers routed the Giants, 37-0, and started the legend of the 1960s Packers growing.

Hornung was named the MVP of the game and was awarded a brand-new Corvette, which he failed to declare on his taxes, even though he claimed the new car was non-taxable because of its "educational, artistic, scientific and civic achievements." The IRS wasn't amused.

But that incident also demonstrated Hornung's relative disregard for authority.

In 1963, at the height of his career and popularity, Hornung was suspended by NFL commissioner Pete Rozelle for gambling and sat out the entire season. In March of 1964, when he was told the suspension was lifted, he called Lombardi to ask when he should report for the team's spring workouts, which were beginning in late April.

Hornung suggested he arrive in early May, just after the Kentucky Derby. Lombardi was not amused.

"Coach said April 15," Hornung recalled. "So we compromised and I was there April 15."

But even after his suspension, Hornung didn't change. Long known as a playboy with his golden hair and rugged good looks, he was one of the great ladies' men and could often be found during the season at a lounge in Appleton, where he wasn't exactly studying his playbook for the next game.

He was fined twice by Lombardi in 1964 for breaking team rules, and one of his quotes seemed to sum up his life: "Never get married in the morning—You never know who you might meet that night."

Ironically, as crucial as Hornung was to the growing Packers dynasty, he never did play in a Super Bowl, though he does own a Super Bowl ring from the first Packers triumph over Kansas City. He didn't play that day because of an injury, and that proved to be his final season.

Paul Hornung had a special relationship with Vince Lombardi, though even Hornung knew not to push the coach too far. *Photo courtesy of Vernon J. Biever*

But Hornung, even though he moved back to his hometown of Louisville, Kentucky, settled down and became a successful businessman, never let the Packers get too far from him.

He often returns to the area for charity functions. For years he did color commentary on Packers preseason games and he will always come back for the annual Packers reunion, where the announcing of his name always gets the loudest ovations from fans.

He even stumped for presidential candidate George W. Bush in 2000, making the rounds of state newspapers all that autumn even though he admitted that he'd never met the man. Nonetheless, just the fact that Paul Hornung was involved was enough for most people.

He was, after all, still the Golden Boy.

Mr. Hutson

The enduring image of Don Hutson was his hands. They were huge. Even by the standards of today's players, Hutson's hands were massive, though soft as a baby's behind.

He caught everything, and in the minds of many, he remains one of the greatest receivers in NFL history even though he retired in 1945. Hutson made the forward pass respectable at a time when the game was still more interested in grinding out yardage on the ground. He brought a combination of grace, athleticism and brute strength to a game that was still viewed as a controlled street brawl in a country where baseball still reigned supreme.

He came out of the University of Alabama in 1935 and showed the NFL things it had never seen before even though most teams passed him up, because at six foot one, 185 pounds they thought he was too fragile to take the poundings of pro football.

But Hutson went on to redefine the wide receiver position and is generally given credit for inventing the concept of pass patterns, whereas before, quarterbacks usually just threw the ball in desperation and hoped someone would catch it.

Packers director of public relations Lee Remmel was just a young reporter for the *Green Bay Press-Gazette* when he saw Hutson for the first, and last, time. It was October

7, 1945, and the Packers were playing in Milwaukee against the Detroit Lions.

In the kind of virtuoso performance Hutson had become famous for, he scored four touchdowns and kicked five extra points—all in the second quarter—and the Packers routed the Lions 57-21. The 29 points in one quarter remains an NFL record.

"It was the most incredible thing I'd ever seen," Remmel said. "I'd never seen him in person before, so this was amazing, and he made it look so effortless."

Hutson retired with 488 receptions and 7,991 yards, and his 99 touchdown receptions remained an NFL record for 44 years until Seattle's Steve Largent broke the mark.

But it was a very different NFL then. Unlike today when teams emphasize the pass over the run almost obsessively and rules changes are designed to benefit the receivers, Hutson played in a league where receivers were fair game, and he understood it only too well.

Hutson can still be found liberally sprinkled throughout the Packers' record book despite the years that have flown by. He still holds the record for years leading the league in receptions, consecutive years leading the league in receptions, most consecutive years leading the team in receiving, most points in a career, most points in a quarter, seasons leading the league in touchdowns, most touchdowns in a career and several others.

When he retired he did what many other former Packers do and stuck around the team. He was an assistant coach under Curly Lambeau for three years and was named to the Packers' board of directors, where he served for another 28 years.

Don Hutson is still considered one of the greatest receivers in NFL history despite the fact that he played his last game in 1945. He still holds numerous Packers team records.
Photo courtesy of Vernon J. Biever

In 1994, when the Packers opened their new indoor practice field, general manager Ron Wolf and president Bob Harlan knew it could be named after only one person, and at its July commemoration, Hutson sheepishly took the platform to accept the honor.

For years, Hutson, who as a player rarely spoke unless spoken to, became an accomplished public speaker.

Inducted into the Pro Football Hall of Fame in 1963, Hutson died June 26, 1997 at the age of 84.

An Era Ends

Simply, the Green Bay Packers likely would not be around today if it weren't for the support, financial and otherwise, from their big brother to the south, Milwaukee.

Logically, the Packers never should have survived in Green Bay anyway. And several times early in the club's history it appeared as if it wouldn't, as money woes descended on the franchise like a swarm of locusts.

The Packers had always looked at Milwaukee with interest, though there were never any serious plans of ever moving the franchise there. These, after all, were the Green Bay Packers and that meant everything. But team officials also knew the state's biggest city could help, not only with growing the fan base but with helping the team's financial bottom line.

As early as 1921, in just the franchise's third season, the Packers played a game at Milwaukee's Borchert Field, tying the Racine Legion team 3-3. The same two teams played there again the following season and then did not go back again until 1933, when an amazing 62-year history began.

From 1933 to 1994, the Packers played at least two games a year in Milwaukee, first at Borchert Field, then in 1952 at Marquette Stadium and for the rest of the time after that at Milwaukee County Stadium, a baseball stadium built for the new Milwaukee Braves that tried to double as a football venue and frequently failed.

But there were good reasons why the Packers tapped into the Milwaukee market. It was a larger market to draw from and meant larger crowds and more revenue. Even more important, playing in Milwaukee thwarted any effort the NFL might use to put a competing franchise 100 miles down the road.

And the relationship between the Packers and Milwaukee flourished. Before long, it just became part of the football season to traipse down to Milwaukee for a Packers game. Milwaukee fans felt a part of the team because they could buy their own package of season tickets, and Green Bay fans dealt with it because they knew it was best for the franchise as a whole.

But it was never easy, especially in later years when the games were played in tiny, cramped, crumbling County Stadium. It was never meant for football, and during Packers games in September, when the baseball season was still under way, the players would find themselves having to play on half a field of infield dirt.

It was also a goofy configuration of the field itself, so that there was little room beyond either end zone, and if a pass went long and a receiver didn't stop, he could end up in the front row with the fans and the popcorn.

As well, the sight lines, which were fine for baseball, were terrible for football. Indeed, the Packers learned from painful experience that if the two teams were on separate sidelines, fans on one side couldn't see the game. That forced both teams onto the same sideline, and it proved uncomfortable for each because now two sets of players, often in a maddened rage, would be mingling far too closely together.

Then there were the ancient locker rooms that were too small for the 25 players on a baseball team and positively agonizing for the 45 on a football team. And in the 1990s, when the Packers were beginning their ascent, the media horde covering the team grew. So after a game, you can only imagine how crowded it was with media, players, coaches and equipment all milling around for a little space to call their own.

And the head coach's postgame press conference? It was held in the baseball weight room next to free weights, barbells and running machines.

And the only thing that made it bearable for the Packers was the knowledge that the visitor's locker room was even worse. It actually got to a point that when the league schedule was announced every year, opposing teams breathed a sigh of relief when they learned they weren't playing at County Stadium.

There was also the basic problem of transportation. Many Packers didn't even look at Milwaukee as a home game because it meant getting on a bus the day before, moving all the gear down the road and staying in a hotel before taking another bus to the game. That sounded to many players an awful lot like a road game, and they already had plenty of those. It was inconvenient and it was a pain and the Packers hated playing down there almost as much as any opposing team.

But probably all of those inconveniences could have been dealt with in some way. What the Packers couldn't ignore was that with every game played at the 53,000-seat stadium, they were losing $1 million. For a franchise like the Packers, that was serious money.

Though they owed a debt to the fans of Milwaukee, the franchise had to be realistic. If they stayed in Milwaukee, they would continue to lose money, and that was an occurrence that team president Bob Harlan couldn't abide.

So in one of the major and most controversial decisions of his presidency, he announced in the spring of 1994 that the Packers would be pulling out of Milwaukee after that season and would play every game in the larger, more spacious and lucrative Lambeau Field.

Naturally, the decision enraged Packers fans in Milwaukee, many of whom had grown up watching the Packers there and assumed it was just the way it would always be. Many felt betrayed, many were angry and they swore to never, ever follow the Packers again.

But Harlan masterfully defused the situation by offering three games a year to current County Stadium season ticket holders. The particular games would be pre-selected before the schedule ever came out so that the Milwaukee fans stood an excellent chance of seeing quality games.

For example, Milwaukee season ticket holders would get home games two, five and seven so that there would be no charges of favoritism that Green Bay fans would get the better games. The plan has worked splendidly, and while Milwaukee fans have to drive 90 minutes north, many have made it a weekend adventure.

In fact, more often than not, Milwaukee fans have been louder and more enthusiastic than the games Green Bay fans attend because, in the words of one Milwaukee fan, we appreciate it more.

That final season at County Stadium was an interesting one. The Packers were clearly building something under Mike Holmgren, and 1994 was another step in that process.

But in the first County Stadium game that year, the Packers played perhaps one of the five worst games ever under Holmgren. Uninspired and unemotional, the Packers fell behind the Miami Dolphins 24-0 before scoring two meaningless fourth-quarter touchdowns.

Afterward, Holmgren stormed into the weight room/ press room, glared at the media and demanded to know if there were any questions. His answers were uncharacteristically short and sarcastic and after a short time, he marched out again and could be heard, even in the din of the cramped locker room and behind closed doors, roaring in frustration.

The second game was a piece of work as well. The Packers built a 31-0 lead on the Detroit Lions and then had to hold on for dear life as the Lions battled back to within 38-30 and had a chance to win in the final minute before a Packers defensive stand.

That the final Packers game ever at County Stadium was just as memorable was no surprise. It was played December 18 against the Atlanta Falcons and would go down as one of the more exciting games played not only in Milwaukee but in the storied Packers annals.

Trailing the Falcons deep in the fourth quarter and with a playoff berth on the line, Brett Favre drove the Packers 67 yards in the final 1:58, completing six of nine passes and capping the drive with a nine-yard dive into the end zone for the winning score.

After the game, numerous players, many of whom had complained bitterly about playing in Milwaukee, saluted and waved to the crowd.

It was the end of an era, but what a way to end it.

Ryan Longshot

That probably should have been his real name when he stepped onto the scene at training camp in 1997. But Ryan Longwell proved that he was far more than that.

He is one of those great NFL success stories, one of those players who proved to others who don't think they belong that maybe they really do.

He came to Packers training camp completely unknown, a kicker who was cut by the San Francisco 49ers in July and signed the next day by Green Bay because they needed a "camp leg." To those unfamiliar with the jargon, that's a player signed for little other reason than to give the regular kicker a break during practice.

It's a job most kickers understand. They know they won't get a shot with that team, but they know if they do well that other teams in need of a kicker will keep them in mind down the road. It's a risky proposition but really the only one aspiring kickers have.

In Longwell's case, he was the camp leg for Brett Conway, whom the Packers had expended a third-round draft pick on to replace the departed Chris Jacke. Conway came to the Packers with exceptional credentials. He had been successful at a big-time college program, Penn State, and general manager Ron Wolf always liked to draft players from national powerhouses.

So Conway would slip into Jacke's spot and the Packers would be set at placekicker for the next decade. The only problem with that plan was that it never materialized.

Conway struggled in mini-camps and again in training camp, so the Packers kept Longwell around—just in case. After less than impressive performances in the first two preseason games, Conway found himself pressing as the Packers went to Oakland for another preseason game. But as he warmed up, Conway severely pulled a thigh muscle in his kicking leg, forcing the Packers to go with the untested Longwell.

In his first-ever NFL field goal attempt, the free agent from the University of California shanked a 26-yarder. But the Raiders were called for a penalty and Longwell got another chance, this time hitting from 21 yards. The butterflies were gone, and Longwell hit two more field goals that game.

When Conway's injury refused to heal, the Packers placed him on injured reserve, ending his season and giving the job to Longwell for the year.

It wasn't the situation coach Mike Holmgren wanted, especially a job as crucial as that. But the kid had shown him something. He battled through adversity and uncertainty and had never accepted his lot as a kicker with nothing to play for. With every opportunity he'd been given, he'd come through, and that was more than he could say for the high-priced draft choice whose job it was to lose.

Longwell proved to be spectacular. He made all three field goals in the season opener and made three more in Philadelphia before missing a 28-yarder at the end of the game that would have given Green Bay the win. But he shook that off and made 24 of 30 field goals (of the six he missed, two were blocked and two hit the uprights) for the season and all 48 extra points.

In the postseason, he made seven of eight field goals, and none was bigger than a 43-yarder in the wind and rain of the NFC title game against San Francisco in Candlestick Park just before halftime that gave the Packers a 10-point lead.

Since then, he has become another Packers institution. With his gee-willikers attitude and his accessibility to the fans and media, he's become another favorite in Green Bay. He has never taken himself too seriously and even when he's struggled, as he did in 2001, he has always maintained the right attitude.

He now ranks as the fifth most accurate kicker in NFL history. Not bad for a camp leg.

A Rocky Rhodes

Today Ron Wolf admits he made a huge mistake in moving too quickly to replace Holmgren. But at the time, with nerves raw and with a need to make a decisive decision, he was convinced he'd found his man in Ray Rhodes.

Rhodes was one of those tough-as-nails guys Wolf was convinced the Packers needed, especially after the 1998 season when it appeared to him that Holmgren's message was no longer getting through.

That's where Rhodes came in. He had everything Wolf was looking for in a head coach. He had NFL head coaching experience with Philadelphia, having led the

Eagles to a playoff berth in 1997 and earning NFC Coach of the Year honors. He was a tough guy, a no-nonsense butt-kicker who had none, and wanted none, of the glamour that went along with being head coach of the Packers.

And he knew Green Bay after spending two years as Holmgren's defensive coordinator when he first came to the Packers.

All the stars seemed aligned when Wolf went after Rhodes, who had just been released by the Eagles. So sure was Wolf, in fact, that he never even interviewed any other candidates for the job, including offensive coordinator Sherman Lewis, who desperately wanted the job and felt, not without reason, that he'd earned it.

Looking back, Wolf now knows he should have taken more time to look for a coach and study the troubling signs that should have warned him off Rhodes.

"I moved too fast," Wolf said. "But I thought Ray was everything we were looking for."

In fact, Rhodes's last season in Philly was a struggle. His players fell away as the season bottomed out, and he didn't help himself by comparing the thought of losing to having a burglar break into his home and rape and kill his wife and daughters.

There was also the persistent rumor that Rhodes hated the two years he was in Green Bay. Though Rhodes denied it, it was well known that Rhodes and his family had trouble assimilating in a town with only a handful of African Americans. It was not Philadelphia or San Francisco, his previous stops, or New York, where he'd played for so many years.

Green Bay, Wisconsin was what it was, and it never pretended to be anything else. But it was difficult for

Rhodes, especially since he was hearing the call of head coaching himself and wasn't sure he'd ever get a chance, or even wanted a chance, with the Packers. So after two seasons, just when Holmgren was beginning to put the pieces together, Rhodes bolted, angering the head coach and leading to what was a long rift between the two.

Ironically, after the 2002 season, Holmgren rehired Rhodes as his defensive coordinator in Seattle.

All those signs probably should have slowed Wolf's thought processes, but they didn't. Instead, Rhodes quickly accepted the job and made it clear he wasn't going to necessarily fix what wasn't broken. He compared the Packers to an older car that just needed a few spark plugs and an oil change and would be as good as new.

It wasn't quite that simple, however. Despite an unbeaten preseason that gave the impression all was well, problems bubbled just below the surface. In a preseason win over the Denver Broncos in Madison, Wisconsin, quarterback Brett Favre suffered what was called at the time a sprained thumb on his right hand. But Favre, who had laughed off injuries his entire career, made it clear that this one worried him. He was knocked to the ground by Broncos linebacker John Mobley, and Favre used his right hand to cushion the blow. As he hit the hard, unforgiving Camp Randall Stadium turf, his thumb bent back painfully, and he was convinced the thumb was broken.

He left that game and did not play the rest of the preseason to rest the injury, but while it improved, it was a source of concern all season.

In the regular-season opener at Lambeau Field, Favre was his usual gritty self, engineering two scoring drives in the final eight minutes to beat the Oakland Raiders.

Afterward, in an emotional display that caught nearly everyone off guard, Favre broke down and cried during his postgame press conference. For Favre, all the frustration, all the pain, all the uncertainty came to the surface and there was nowhere for it to go.

He missed Holmgren more than he ever let on. Reggie White, who had come to Green Bay just to play with Favre, had retired. The world he knew was changing, and he wasn't sure if it was for the better.

He got an answer several weeks later when the Packers were blown out by the Broncos in Denver. It was a 31-10 loss in which Favre played perhaps the worst game of his pro career.

On the grim plane ride back, Favre sat next to Wolf to let him know he wasn't happy with the direction of the team. Insult was added to injury two weeks later when Holmgren brought his new team, the Seahawks, to Lambeau Field and routed the Packers, 27-7, in front of a Monday night TV crowd.

It was a season that saw the Packers lose an incredible three home games after it had taken them four seasons to lose that many at Lambeau Field prior to that. And while it was bad enough to lose to the Chicago Bears in front of the home folks, the final proof for Wolf that he'd made the wrong decision came when the Packers dropped a crucial December 12 game to the Carolina Panthers.

In that game, Rhodes refused to call any of three timeouts he had remaining as the Panthers drove relentlessly downfield for the winning score. The Panthers waited for the clock to run down, called their own timeout and scored on the game's last play to pull out the 33-31 win.

Wolf watched Rhodes's coaching blunder in stunned disbelief. Then after the game, Rhodes tried to explain the gaffe by saying he wanted the give the defense a chance to make a stand and stop the drive. It was bizarre logic, and Wolf knew he'd made a mistake.

He also knew when he'd attend practices late in the season and saw how undisciplined the team was. It reminded him all too uncomfortably of 1991 when, as the new GM, he'd attended the practices of then coach Lindy Infante. He told team president Bob Harlan then that the Packers had a problem. Wolf knew he had the same problem now.

After the Packers beat the Arizona Cardinals to close out the season at 8-8, Wolf had already made his decision that Rhodes had to go. Even though the Packers weren't eliminated from the playoffs until later in the day when the Cowboys defeated the Giants, Wolf had made up his mind.

The man he thought could bring discipline and toughness back to the Packers wasn't the same man who stepped on the sidelines in 1999. Whether his experience in Philadelphia had changed him or whether he just couldn't stoke the fire in Green Bay, Rhodes had changed from the taskmaster Wolf had hoped for.

The night after the last game, Wolf brought Rhodes into his office and fired him. Veteran safety LeRoy Butler, one of the players Wolf listened to when he said the situation was deteriorating, was nonetheless shocked by Rhodes's firing.

"I guess he knows what he's doing," Butler said of Wolf. "But one year? Man, that's tough."

But Wolf had also sent a message that even one year away from the playoffs was not acceptable—at least not for this franchise.

In replacing Rhodes, Wolf vowed to take his time and make the right choice based on what was best for the Packers' present and future. The decision to hire Mike Sherman, a relative unknown, sent shockwaves through the NFL and Green Bay. But it was a decision Wolf knew he could defend. Mike Sherman would prove Wolf still knew what he was doing.

Terrible Tony

H e was the next-generation offensive lineman. At 6'6", 325 pounds, Tony Mandarich was the prototypical tackle, the player who would make whatever team drafted him an immediate force. Quick, big, strong and smart, Mandarich had suddenly made every other offensive lineman obsolete.

And in 1989, the Green Bay Packers had to have him.

The Packers were spinning their wheels mightily when that draft came. Lindy Infante had just finished his first season as head coach, and the Packers responded with a 4-12 season that was only that good because the Packers won their final two games.

But that was going to change in 1989 and Mandarich, the behemoth from Michigan State, was going to be the cornerstone.

Picking second in that draft, the argument was whether the Packers should draft Mandarich, the sure-thing tackle, or take a flier on a quarterback from UCLA on whom the jury was still out—Troy Aikman. But with the Packers' braintrust, led by player personnel director Tom Braatz, there was really no question who that pick would be. The Packers had focused, almost obsessively, on Mandarich, and when the time came to pick, they wasted no time. Aikman? He went to the Dallas Cowboys later and, oh yeah, won three Super Bowls.

But the Packers felt they had the player they needed to make that difficult step toward respectability. And when Mandarich showed up at his press unveiling, he drew gasps of awe as his sculpted body barely stayed in the tight-fitting shirt he wore.

He was larger than life and the Packers had made the perfect selection. Or so they thought until they put him in pads and got him on the football field.

The Packers' coaching staff, which had been so anxious to see what their new star could do, found out quickly that he couldn't do much. In fact, the guy who was going to set a new standard for NFL offensive linemen over the next decade couldn't even take the starting right tackle job away from journeyman Alan Veingrad. It became a national story and something of a franchise embarrassment that this incredible hulk couldn't start for a mediocre team.

Unfortunately it got worse for the Packers when the rampant rumors of Mandarich's steroid use started to get a foothold. The NFL was already trying to crack down on the use of illegal muscle-building substances that were proven to cause health problems later in life. Players were routinely, and randomly, tested for steroid use, and the spotlight fell on Mandarich among others around the league.

And while Mandarich never flunked a drug test, or so he claimed, the change in his body was obvious and shocking. Once a chiseled specimen who thought nothing of showing off what he had, he soon grew soft and flabby. And those demonstrations touting his wondrous physique? Those ended, too.

But the Packers had too much time, money and prestige invested in him, and Mandarich finally grabbed the starting right tackle job in 1990, whether he'd really earned it or not.

The results weren't pretty. The nadir came in a December 10 nationally televised game in Philadephia against Randall Cunningham's Eagles. In what many longtime observers consider one of the worst performances in recent history, the Packers barely put up a struggle and were beaten 31-0. What made it worse was how Eagles All-Pro defensive end Reggie White threw Mandarich all over the field as though he was some rag doll.

Eagles defensive tackle Bob Golic had the best line of all when he said he and his teammates would have gotten to Packers quarterback Anthony Dilweg even more if they hadn't kept tripping over Mandarich while on the way to the backfield.

Mandarich held the job most of the next season, Infante's last, before he was plagued by what was diagnosed as a post-concussion syndrome that ended his season. The next year, Mike Holmgren's first, it became obvious the onetime franchise savior no longer fit into the Packers' plans.

Mandarich retired into seclusion in the northern Michigan woods before resurfacing several years later to play left tackle for the woeful Indianapolis Colts. But he was never the player anybody expected he'd be, and Tony Mandarich may go down as the worst No. 1 draft pick in team history.

Unless...

Packers head scout Red Cochrane sat in the team's draft headquarters and begged, literally begged, head coach Bart Starr to draft a quarterback from Notre Dame named Joe Montana. Cochrane saw something special in this kid who had finished an uneven college career with a remarkable comeback win in the Cotton Bowl. He was worth the gamble, worth a third-round draft pick and, frankly, was already better than anything the Packers had at quarterback.

True, Starr had wrangled a deal for Lynn Dickey from Houston and was expected to replace David Whitehurst that season. But no one really knew what to expect from him. Cochrane knew deep down that Montana would be special, especially if given time to refine his considerable gifts.

But Cochrane's words hit a brick wall that day, and in the second round of the draft, Starr drafted a defensive tackle from Maryland, Charles Johnson, who played parts of three seasons for the Packers and amounted to just about nothing.

As for Montana, he was eventually drafted by the San Francisco 49ers, a team desperate for a new direction under new coach Bill Walsh. He was moderately more successful than Johnson. And Red Cochrane, sometimes good-naturedly and sometimes not, never let anyone in the organization forget it.

Another beauty of a miscalculation came in 1983 when the Packers had a chance, late in the draft, to grab a promising nose tackle from Wisconsin named Tim Krumrie. In the 10th round of any draft, the pickings are usually slim, but the Packers could always use defensive line help, and grabbing a state guy was never bad for the organization.

Instead, in another puzzling move that had fans and media alike scratching their heads, the Packers took defensive back Jimmy Thomas from Indiana. The only problem with that was that Thomas wasn't really a defensive back and hadn't played football for a while. Instead, he had played for the Indiana basketball team, but the Packers were intrigued by his athleticism.

He never made the team, and Krumrie would go on to a Pro Bowl career with the Cincinnati Bengals even though his career was cut short with an injury.

And let's not forget the 1991 draft that surely marked the beginning of the end for Lindy Infante and player personnel director Tom Braatz.

Though the draft then didn't demand that first-year players contribute as significantly as it does today, the Packers botched an entire draft and caused reverberations for years.

It began ominously enough when the Packers traded down in the first round, giving their eighth pick overall to Philadelphia and moving down to 19th in the round to grab Ohio State cornerback Vinnie Clark. He couldn't cover anybody and couldn't tackle, and he lasted two seasons.

Oregon State nose tackle Esera Tuaolo was taken in the second round, proved he had a terrific singing voice, and lasted two seasons. In the third round, the Packers went local, drafting Wisconsin defensive end Don Davey, from nearby Manitowoc, who played four decent seasons before moving on. The other third-round pick, Tennessee runningback Chuck Webb, was a head case who showed up overweight for training camp and then simply faded away.

Jeff Fite, a left-footed punter, was the steal of the draft in the fourth round, according to Braatz, but was cut early in training camp. In the sixth round, fullback Walter Dean lasted one season and center Joe Garten left training camp, returned and then was cut.

Of the seven players taken after that, only one made it through training camp and one, 11th-rounder J. J. Wierenga, told the Packers the day after the draft that he wasn't going to play football any more.

The next year, Ron Wolf was in charge.

The Quarterback, Part IV

The belief was that Brett Favre was invincible. He had taken the kind of licks that would make most people weep like children, but he had always come back, better than ever. From ankle sprains and pulled muscles, from sore shoulders and foot injuries, Favre was always there, always performing and never, ever complaining.

In fact, it was Favre's brute determination and toughness that was part of the reason Reggie White decided to cast his free-agency lot with a Packers team that still hadn't proven anything.

White recalled a game in 1992, Favre's seventh career start, when the powerful Eagles went to Milwaukee County Stadium and were upset by the upstart Packers, 27-24. And what impressed White, who already knew he'd probably be leaving the Eagles after the season, was the play of the young pup quarterback. Favre brought the Packers back twice from deficits, completing 23 of 33 passes for 275 yards and two touchdowns, and most of it was done with a painful left shoulder White had helped to injure with a sack.

But White watched in amazement as the kid kept coming back and coming back and never letting the injury keep him down.

"You could see how important the game was to him," White said later. "He was hurt but he wasn't going to let his team lose. I knew that I wanted to play with a guy like that."

But for all of Favre's toughness, there was a price to be paid. It didn't take long for Favre to realize that with the beatings he was taking week in and week out, it was necessary to find some way to relieve that pain to keep going.

For Favre, it ended up being the highly addictive painkiller Vicodin. It was subtle at first, a pill here and there to take the edge off the pain. But eventually, it became every day and all the time. It got so bad at one stage that Favre would take the pills, throw up and then find the capsules in his vomit and swallow them again. That, along with his well-known affection for alcohol, was putting Favre on the fast track toward disaster.

The situation came to a boil in 1996 when a series of events forced Favre to re-examine his life and his approach toward it.

It was a year in which Favre's best friend from Mississippi, Mark Haverty, was killed in a car wreck in which Favre's brother, Scott, was driving. It was a year where Favre's sister, Brandi, was implicated in a drive-by shooting. It was a year that saw Favre's longtime girlfriend,

Deanna, threaten to leave him and take their baby daughter with her if he didn't straighten out.

Finally, in a remarkable May press conference, Favre admitted he had an addiction to painkillers and was going into a Kansas rehab clinic to shake it. It was a stunning revelation to Packers fans and even many within the organization, who had no idea what the quarterback was struggling with.

But even as he agreed to go into treatment, something Favre privately thought he didn't need, the swagger remained. So while pundits and fans alike already wrote off the Packers and Favre, his statement was simple enough: "Don't bet against me."

When Favre re-emerged, he was tightly controlled by coach Mike Holmgren, who didn't want the incident to erupt and ruin what he felt could be a special season for the Packers.

So there was one press conference prior to training camp. One opportunity for reporters to ask about what had happened and what might happen; one chance to get it all out in the open before Holmgren shut the door once and for all.

And when that season began on September 1 in Tampa, the air of anticipation and curiosity was thicker than the humid Florida air. How would Favre respond to all the conjecture? Would he be the same player after rehab he was before? Would he take the chances he once did because of the consequences an injury might bring? And how would the Packers as a team respond to their changed leader?

The answers came quickly and forcefully. At the end of a three-hour dissection of the Buccaneers, Favre completed 20 of 27 passes for 247 yards and four touchdowns as the Packers won 34-3 and were off and winging to a Super Bowl title.

After the game, Favre had the same words for his critics that he'd had for his earlier doubters.

"I never had any doubts," he said. "I told you before, bet against me and you'll lose."

Today, little has changed with the player who is still the most important piece in the Packers' puzzle. He has started an incredible 190 straight games over 11 seasons, a record that will likely never be approached, much less broken. But he has always done more than simply show up and play. He is among the NFL's best ever in yardage, touchdowns and completions and has thrown at least 30 touchdown passes in seven seasons.

And even today, at the relatively advanced football age of 33, Favre is the same player he was when he was 23. A kid at heart, Favre is still known for his locker room antics such as setting off stink bombs and dumping cold water on a teammate as he is relaxing on the porcelain throne.

But Favre also remains a media favorite because of his willingness to talk freely and emotionally and honestly. He perhaps has been a little too honest, especially during the 2002 season when he offered up that he was considering retirement, especially if the Packers won the Super Bowl that year.

They didn't, and Favre has since made it clear retirement is still off in the distance—though not as far as it once was.

He also showed in 2002 how tough he continues to be. In an October 20 game at Lambeau Field against the Redskins, Favre's streak of consecutive starts nearly ended when he was sacked by LaVar Arrington and twisted his knee. In obvious pain, Favre was carted off the field, his head buried in a towel. Fans, and teammates, thought the worst.

Fortunately for Favre and the Packers, the injury, while serious enough, had plenty of time to heal since the Packers had a bye the following week and didn't play until Monday night the week after that. And when the Packers played the Miami Dolphins, Favre, equipped with a bulky knee brace, started and played and led the Packers to a win.

For Brett Favre, the best quarterback this franchise has ever known, it was just another day at the office.

Cowboy Envy

Through most of the mid-1990s, the Packers' greatest rival wasn't the Chicago Bears or Minnesota Vikings. It was the Dallas Cowboys. For a stretch of five years—from 1993-97—the Cowboys tormented the Packers, beating them seven straight times, including three times in the playoffs—one of which was in the NFC title game.

"I don't care what anybody ever says about the Bears; for a while we just hated the Cowboys," safety LeRoy Butler once said.

And with good reason, too. That's because everything the Dallas Cowboys were, the Packers wanted to be. There was envy and anger and longing and a wonder on the Packers' part if they'd ever get to the point where the Cowboys were.

The Cowboys were polished and confident to the point of arrogance. They had playmakers on offense, a great defense and, perhaps most important, they knew what it took to win the games they had to win.

That's what the Packers first noticed in 1993 when they went to Texas Stadium for their first playoff game in 11 years and were beaten by the Cowboys, who were beginning their run of three Super Bowl titles in four years. It wasn't as though the Cowboys embarrassed the Packers, because the final score was only 27-17. But there was never a moment, not once in the entire game, where the Packers thought they could win the game. The Cowboys controlled it from beginning to end, and in the long run, the Packers were little more to them than a bug to be flicked off a shirt.

The next year it was no different. In fact, it was worse. In the Thanksgving Day game in Dallas, the Packers faced a depleted Cowboys team that was without quarterback Troy Aikman and backup Rodney Peete. So No. 3 quarterback Jason Garrett threw for more than 300 yards and three touchdowns and rallied the Cowboys to a 42-31 win that was embarrassing. Two months later, the Packers had to go back to Dallas for another playoff game and were routed again, 35-9.

With four losses in two years, and none of them especially close, the Cowboys were becoming a phobia to the Packers, and it was something coach Mike Holmgren had to alleviate. But how?

He knew the Cowboys were quicker and he knew they played better on artificial turf. Holmgren also knew that if he could get the Cowboys up on the real grass at Lambeau, especially in November or December, the results would be different.

Instead, the Packers lost another regular-season game in Dallas in 1995 and had to go back there for the NFC championship game for the right to go to the Super Bowl.

This time, it looked like it might be different. The uncertain Packers of 1993 were gone, replaced by the kind of talented and confident crew that could take the Cowboys head on.

And heading into the fourth quarter, the Packers led the Cowboys and seemed on the verge of taking the next step toward dominance, until Brett Favre threw a costly interception and the Cowboys rallied for two touchdowns and the win.

This one hurt more than all the others combined, because the Packers knew in their hearts they were as good as, if not better than, the Cowboys. So as the victors celebrated on the Texas Stadium turf, every Packer made a solemn pledge to remember how this felt and to never let it happen again.

Even on the flight back to Green Bay afterward, Holmgren went up and down the aisle of the airplane telling his players to remember and use it as a rallying cry.

And that's exactly how the Packers went into the 1996 season. Ironically, the Packers again had to travel to Texas for a Monday night game, but this time they were without three of their best receivers. The offense could mount little and the defense played hard, holding the Cowboys to seven Chris Boniol field goals, a club record. The Packers still lost 21-6, and it got ugly at the end when the Cowboys kicked a late field goal to give Boniol the record.

After the kick, several Packers, led by of all people Reggie White, got into a shoving match with several Cowboys because of what Green Bay saw as piling it on. It was just another chapter in a simmering, growing rivalry.

But the Packers knew 1996 was their season and they knew, or at least they hoped, to get the Cowboys into frigid Lambeau in the playoffs to exact some long-sought revenge.

Unfortunately for the Packers and their hungry fans, the Carolina Panthers spoiled the plans by upsetting the Cowboys in the playoffs and earning a meeting with Green Bay in the NFC title game.

Even the Panthers knew how badly the Packers wanted the Cowboys.

"Sorry," said Panthers quarterback Kerry Collins. "I know you guys wanted the Cowboys, but we're here instead."

But time moves on and personnel changes and players get older. In 1997, the NFL schedule-makers finally sent the Cowboys to Green Bay for a regular-season game in November. And while it wasn't a playoff game and the Cowboys clearly weren't the same team they'd been, the Packers rolled to a 45-17 victory that went a long way to healing the wounds of the previous years.

Still, the rivalry had changed. The two teams were passing each other in opposite directions, and it was no longer as fun as it once was. Just as ironically, since 1997, the two teams have played each other just once. Maybe the NFL realized the rivalry had cooled, too.

Those Fans

In the end, it still comes down to the fans. It begins and ends there. It always has and it always will. To the uninitiated players, the traits they see in Green Bay Packers fans are obsessive, loyal, often obnoxious, sometimes ridiculous, but always there when the team needs them most. It is almost a cult in blaze orange, and the only people who don't understand who Packers fans are and why they do what they do would never understand the explanation anyway.

Consider Mike Flanagan, the versatile Packers offensive lineman who, as a rookie, saw 5,000 attend the opening day of training camp. He turned to a fellow rookie and said, "Don't these people have jobs?"

But Flanagan soon understood what the devotion was all about. Sure, a lot of it has to do with the fact that Green Bay isn't exactly Midtown Manhattan—there isn't a whole lot going on, especially in the winter.

But it's more than that. Packers fans understand better than many fans in other NFL cities how important it is to have a pro football team. They know that, by anything resembling logic, there shouldn't be a pro franchise of any kind in a city this size. But here it is and here it will stay, and fans guard this franchise the way a mother lion protects her cub.

The Packers survive on a knife's edge. With an NFL-mandated salary cap and revenue sharing, much of it coming with lucrative TV deals, the Packers are able to compete with the New York Giants and Dallas Cowboys and Washington Redskins.

But as everyone involved with the Packers likes to say over and over and over again, there is no single owner who can take money from one of his other businesses and throw it into his struggling football team. The Packers live and die by the money supplied from the league, from the TV and radio deals, and from merchandising. That's why the $295 million renovation of Lambeau Field was so crucial to the team's survival. Now there's an opportunity to use the stadium year-round for various events that will supply more money to the franchise.

But it will always be a struggle for the Packers, and if there ever does come a day when the team simply can't survive, its end has already been decided. For years, it was written into the team by-laws that if the franchise folded, any money remaining after debts were paid off would go the local Green Bay VFW post.

But more recently, as times and priorities have changed, the by-laws were rewritten, and now in such a case, any money left over would go to The Green Bay Packers Foundation, a group that disperses money to local charities. So, really, even if there are no more Green Bay Packers as a team, they will live on in some small way.

All Packers know this. They know the history of the team, they swear that either they were at Ice Bowl or a relative was, and everyone has a memory burned into their brains about this team.

They are indeed loyal, almost to a fault. But they're not blindly loyal and they're not stupid. Every game has been sold out since 1960, but that doesn't mean every game has had every seat filled.

Take, for example, the surreal setting that was the 1987 season when NFL players walked out on strike and replacement teams were quickly cobbled together. These were teams made up of has-beens and never-weres. They were players literally pulled off the street from their jobs as computer analysts or truck drivers. They were placed in pro football games, and, for most of them, it was the greatest time of their lives.

But Packers fans understood what they were, and weren't. Attendance at the two games played at Lambeau Field numbered around 35,000 for a stadium that seated nearly 60,000. But while many fans stayed away, that attendance was among the highest for any replacement games.

And those Packers, who were quarterbacked by a guy named Alan Risher and who were led by a safety named Jim Bob Morris, managed to catch the fancy of dubious fans.

The Packers went 2-1 in the replacement games, and their enthusiasm and earnestness in playing won over a lot of people. They grew to realize that, for these guys, just playing the game was enough. In many respects, those replacements played harder than the real thing.

It's why 45,000 people will show up for a Packers training camp intrasquad game and wait four hours in brutal cold and snow to welcome the team back from their Super Bowl XXXI triumph.

They have always considered themselves different from other football fans and, really, different from most sports fans in general. And while their antics can border on the obnoxious, when the game is on the line, Packers fans are always there.

But it's also why they know right from wrong, too.

Many times over the years, they have voiced their displeasure, their frustation, their anger and their disappointment in a team they have staked just about everything on.

One time in the 1991 season, the last under Lindy Infante, the Packers played a Thursday night nationally televised game against the Chicago Bears, a game that should have brought the best out in the Packers. Instead, it brought out nothing at all.

The Packers did nothing offensively, played uninspired on defense, made mistakes more characteristic of a high school team and lost a yawner, 10-0.

As the players skulked off the field afterward, they were bombarded by a torrent of expletives few had ever from Packers fans before. In fact, to some observers, it was the worst barrage of language and invective any had ever heard before.

"I guess we deserved it," quarterback Don Majkowski said at the time.

Packers fans also rose up in arms for what they saw as a perceived slight of two players who helped Green Bay to a Super Bowl title in 1996. After winning the championship, the Packers were invited to the White House to schmooze with President Clinton. Nearly every player and coach attended—except famously conservative tight end Mark Chmura who had no intention of being honored by a Democratic president, and two other players, wide receiver Andre Rison and kicker Chris Jacke.

And when the Packers held a ritzy ceremony at the swanky Oneida Golf and Country Club to receive their Super Bowl rings later that summer, again Rison and Jacke weren't invited.

The team's stated reason for leaving those two out was, in their view, quite simple. Neither was going to be with the team the following season because both were free agents that the team had no intention of signing. As a result, if you're not on the team, you're not part of the celebration. It didn't mean they wouldn't get their rings, it just meant they'd get them in the mail.

It seemed like a cheap and sleazy stunt and when word leaked out of the slight, many Packers fans agreed. Both had played big roles in the Super Bowl win and both were key factors all season in getting the Packers to that point.

Jacke won the scintillating Monday night game over San Francisco with a 53-yard field goal in overtime and hit 21 of 27 field goals for the season. Rison came in at a critical juncture midway through the season when the Packers were desperate for a receiver. He provided a cushion when they needed it most, and his touchdown reception in the opening minutes of the Super Bowl set the tone for the game.

But they were suddenly persona non pigskin around Packers headquarters, and that struck too many people as petty.

It was an incident that wounded the Packers' pride and took a long time to mend. But coach Mike Holmgren, for one, made no apologies.

Never a huge fan of Jacke's anyway, Holmgren tolerated him because of his penchant for making the big kick at the right time. But he also viewed Jacke as selfish and self-centered. The stories were rampant of Jacke calling to sell Super Bowl tickets minutes after winning the NFC championship game and, after the Super Bowl, how he'd arranged to fly back to Green Bay separately from the team flight.

But Rison was different. Long labeled a malcontent with every team he'd been with, he came to Green Bay and truly believed he'd found a home. He developed a quick rapport with quarterback Brett Favre, the same guy he'd called a "hillbilly" the year before when Rison played in Cleveland. It was a remark Favre reveled in and responded to by saying, "He's right." But in Green Bay, Rison had hoped he'd made his last NFL stop.

"I really feel like I belong here," he said.

But the Packers felt differently, and in the rugged world of pro football, the team had to decide between Rison or long-time Packers receiver Robert Brooks, who missed the last half of the '96 season with a disastrous knee injury. Convinced Brooks could come back and willing to reward him for years of service, the Packers cut Rison loose and Brooks was given a new five-year, $15 million contract.

It didn't work as the Packers had hoped. Though Brooks responded in 1997 with 60 catches and 1,010 yards, he had lost the explosive breakaway speed that had been his trademark. After another injury-filled year in 1998, Brooks called it quits.

And Rison, who had hoped to stick in Green Bay, moved on again, while Jacke's NFL career continued when he signed with the Arizona Cardinals in 1997.

But the annoyance with the Packers over that decision was short-lived, as it usually is when there are disagreements. After all, there was a new season to prepare for.

Reggie in
Black and White

No one will ever take away what Reggie White meant to the Green Bay Packers in the six years he played for them. Not only was he a major part of the Packers' rise to prominence in the mid- to late '90s, he was an ambassador for Wisconsin.

It was an odd pairing, really. The fervently religious White, an ordained minister from Tennessee living in

Chris Jacke was a superb kicker for the Packers from 1989-96, but he alienated teammates and coaches on occasion with his sometimes selfish behavior. *Photo courtesy of Vernon J. Biever*

Northeast Wisconsin, where the black population could almost be counted on one hand. But White did his ministry work as he promised he would, going down to Milwaukee and working with the disadvantaged youth there. He was true to his word on many aspects of what he said he would do when he signed with the Packers.

But as many people learned over the years, Reggie was Reggie—a puzzling amalgam of contradictions who could be infuriating and engaging, almost at the same time.

He was fond of telling cynics that he had no problem preaching love and kindness off the field while trying to tear off a quarterback's head on the field. He had no problem railing publicly against homosexuality and promiscuousness even to the embarrassment, sometimes, of the Packers organization.

In one particularly memorable oration, at a packed press conference prior to the 1995 NFC title game in Dallas, White called for the suspension of the U.S. Constitution when it came to following God's law, leaving some media types with their mouths hanging open.

The next year, the church where he ministered in Knoxville, Tennessee was burned to ground in an act of vandalism. Shaken and angry, White vowed to rebuild the church, and the people of Wisconsin answered the call, donating more than $100,000 to help the cause.

White broke down in tears and spoke movingly as he accepted the donation. Unfortunately, the goodwill has dissipated, since the church was never rebuilt and no one seems to know what happened to the money—including White.

Several years later, he attacked homosexuality, prompting comments from, among others, Minnesota Vikings Robert Smith, who told White to shut up about subjects he knew nothing about. There was also the incident when White spoke to the Wisconsin Assembly in Madison and went off on a tangent about how Mexicans were good at making large families and the Japanese could do wonders with clock radios while the lawmakers squirmed uneasily in their seats.

In White's mind, there was nothing wrong with what he said. His world was, and remains, black and white. There is right and wrong and very little in between. And when his comments caused a firestorm of controversy, he seemed not to understand why.

He would talk passionately and at length about kids and the need for education, especially in the black community, but sometimes he didn't practice what he preached.

One observer remembers going to White's house early one weekday morning. As his school-aged kids rolled out of bed, having overslept and in danger of being late for school, White told his kids just to stay home instead of going in late. And this was even with the White house directly abutting the school his kids went to, meaning no more than a two-minute walk.

But that's Reggie.

It even carried over to his final Packers game, an emotional and memorable day on December 20, 1998 against the Tennessee Oilers when he circled Lambeau Field in the snow to salute the fans.

But that memory didn't last as, a year later, he decided he wasn't ready to retire and signed with the Carolina Panthers for a less than memorable season that many viewed as nothing more than a chance for him to pad his quarterback sack statistics.

Eventually, even he realized it was enough and quit for good. He remains a beloved figure in Green Bay for what he helped bring to the Packers. But there will always be a segment that never quite knew what to make of him. And maybe that's exactly the way he always wanted it.

Mr. Starr

Bart Starr will always have a special place in the hearts of Packers fans—as a player, as a coach, and still as an ambassador for the Packers and what they mean to so many people.

He was the quarterback of those remarkable teams in the 1960s that won five NFL titles. He was unflappable, unbreakable and unbeatable, even if he never put up what might be considered eye-popping statistics today. But he played 16 years and 196 games, both club marks that still stand, and he trails only the prolific Brett Favre in most other quarterback categories.

No one embodied the Packers more, so maybe it was no surprise that he would become the head coach and, at least for a few years, the general manager as well. And maybe it's a testament to his stature that even after nine years as head coach in which he produced just two winning seasons and one playoff berth, his stature remains monumental.

What made Starr loved by his players was his desire to protect them from the ills of the outside world, especially the media. That's when Starr would lose his gentlemanly nature and blow up. Starr did have a temper, and it would often flash when a player was brought under scrutiny.

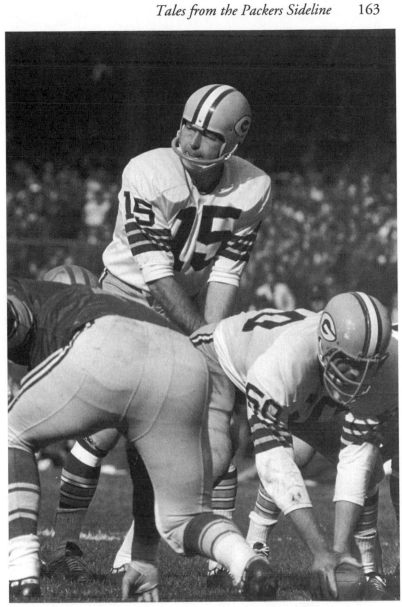

Bart Starr remains one of the icons in team history. A two-time Super Bowl MVP, he returned to Green Bay as head coach and general manager and never recaptured the success. But he remains beloved even today. *Photo courtesy of Vernon J. Biever*

Usually if Starr had a problem with the way the media presented a situation, he would call the offending journalist into his office and make his point the old-fashioned way. But he would start by having the reported sit in a low-riding couch where his knees would wind up around his nostrils. And Starr would sit behind his huge desk, looking down imperiously at the offender. It was an effective strategy and probably one he learned from his mentor, Vince Lombardi.

After the 1983 season, Starr was fired as head coach, and he slipped into private life where he continued to extol the virtues of the Packers.

And if any situation marks what Starr was like, consider the 1997 Super Bowl in San Diego. Starr was eating lunch with friends at an outdoor restaurant when fans began to trickle by. Soon the trickle became a torrent, and fans surrounded his table seeking autographs. Starr paused, put down his knife and fork, and calmly explained that he was eating and when was through he'd be glad to sign.

The fans waited and, as soon as lunch was done, he indeed sat and signed autographs for an hour. That's Bart Starr—then, now and forever.

The Quarterback,
Part V

It's just a simple story but maybe one that best encapsulates Brett Favre and his relationship to the community.

For several years his daughter Brittany played on a soccer team for the Green Bay parochial school she attended. On game days, Favre and his wife would drive up, take out a couple of chairs, sit and watch their daughter play soccer—just like normal parents. And here's the amazing part. They were never bothered by autograph seekers or giggling hangers-on. No one would come up and try to have photos taken with the famous quarterback and no one wanted to discuss why he threw into triple coverage against the Vikings last season.

There, he was just Brett Favre who had a daughter on the soccer team like everyone else. There were no bodyguards around to protect him and no TV cameras.

It was just a quiet time for Favre and his family, and the people who knew him and had seen him around knew to respect that. No one told them to, they just ... knew it.

It has been a remarkable transformation for the former wild child from Kiln, Mississippi, who used to never meet a party he didn't like. The stories, real and imagined, about Favre and his early antics are legendary throughout Green Bay and the surrounding Fox Valley.

"If half those stories were true," Favre said with a smile, "I'd probably be dead by now."

But Favre has never denied or made apologies for his past. He is who he is and he said as much in a defiant press conference after he returned from drug rehab in 1996. Indeed, after the Packers won Super Bowl XXXI, Favre could be found prowling the notorious French Quarter in New Orleans.

But times change and people mature. And Favre is no different.

Certainly the drug rehab changed his view of the world. Certainly so did the ultimatum from his then girlfriend and now wife, Deanna, to straighten up and fly right or she would leave. But probably the biggest changes came after the birth of his daughter Breleigh in 1999. Born premature, Breleigh struggled initially before growing strong and healthy, and that affected Favre profoundly.

So too did a tornado that roared through his Mississippi estate in the spring of 2001. As he crouched in a shed as the storm blew over, protecting Breleigh, he realized there was a lot more to life than just football.

Today, Favre is a different man, a different player, a different person than he was when he blew into town in 1992, unknown and unappreciated.

In the 2002 season, in what many consider his best season ever, Favre led the Packers to a 12-5 season while throwing to a completely revamped group of wide receivers. Instead of longtime companions like Antonio Freeman, Bill Schroeder and Corey Bradford, Favre had to break in new guys like Donald Driver, Robert Ferguson and Terry Glenn and responded by throwing for nearly 4,000 yards.

"No. 4 [Favre] means everything to that team," said longtime linebacker Brian Noble. "If you had put him in with those teams in 1980s, it would have changed everything. That's how much he means."

But Favre is also looking to the future without football, and he began making the Packers nervous in 2002 by dropping more than a few hints about retirement. And it's clear that Favre will not be one of those quarterbacks who hangs around until he's 40 just to stay on a roster.

His creed has always been simple enough. He will retire as a Green Bay Packer and he will go out, he hopes, on his terms and not because injury or poor play has dictated it.

"I'll know when it's time," he said.

And it will be a time Packers fans will dread.

Ezra

Perhaps one of the most misunderstood, and underappreciated, players in team history might have been defensive end Ezra Johnson.

Certainly not huge by the standard of today's player, Johnson was nonetheless one of the best pass rushers this franchise has ever seen, a sackmaster before the sack became such a dominant league statistic.

A 1977 second-round draft pick from Morris Brown College, he is still the only Packer with five sacks in a game and his 20.5 sacks in 1978 remains a club record.

And while many, perhaps most, people remember Johnson for his infamous hot dog munching incident on the sidelines during a preseason game in 1980, former Packers linebacker Brian Noble remembers a quiet, fierce competitor who never got a chance to prove to the rest of the league what a talent he truly was.

One of Noble's most vivid memories of Johnson came when Noble was a hot-headed rookie in 1985 who was unaccustomed to losing.

"Everybody's at their locker after another loss and I come in and I'm just livid about losing," he said. "I was so upset that I threw my helmet and it caught Ezra right in the chest. I went from complete rage to total fear in a matter of seconds. I thought he was going to kill me. But in his deep voice he just said, 'Nobes, we're all upset, and you don't have to be throwing stuff.' That's the last time I did that."

Big Returns

His was a brief, but remarkable, time in Green Bay. He was here and, before we knew it, he was already gone, and there are times we wonder if he was ever here at all. But Desmond Howard was indeed a Packer and one of the main reasons they went on to win a Super Bowl in 1996.

The story is known to all by now, though few remember he was within a day, perhaps hours, of never being a Packer at all.

Howard came to Green Bay with a view that it might be his last chance to stay in the league. He was the celebrated Heisman Trophy-winning wide receiver out of Michigan, blessed with a thousand-watt smile, good speed, and decent hands but absolutely no ability to get off the line of scrimmage against tough coverage.

He was a first-round draft pick of the Washington Redskins but never lived up to his billing there and left to play for the expansion Jacksonville Jaguars, which didn't work out either.

In 1996, with no other teams exactly beating his door down for his services, Howard signed relatively late with the Packers in hopes of finding, perhaps, a slot as a No. 6 receiver or, just maybe, as a return man.

But Howard's luck just didn't seem to hold as he suffered a hip injury early in training camp and saw no practice time, much less game experience.

The Packers' coaches were frustrated because they wanted to see what Howard could do, but injuries kept him off the field. Finally, he was told he wouldn't make it through the first round of cuts if he didn't get out there and show the coaches what he could do.

Then came the second preseason game at Lambeau Field against Pittsburgh and Howard got his chance. He returned a punt for a touchdown and had several other strong returns that opened enough eyes to allow him to earn a roster spot and take over the primary kick return duties.

What happened after that was the stuff of legend. Howard went on to set a club record with 875 punt return yards, and he brought three punts back for touchdowns. In the playoffs, he returned one punt for a touchdown and nearly had a second one in the mire and misery at Lambeau Field against the 49ers.

Then, of course, came the Super Bowl where his 99-yard kickoff return for a touchdown in the third quarter turned the momentum back to the Packers and sealed the win. He finished with 244 return yards and was named the game's MVP.

But as with many things, Howard's success went to his head, and instead of staying with the Packers, he took the big money of free agency and moved on to the Oakland Raiders, where he was assured he would get the chance to prove himself as a legitimate NFL receiver.

Alas for him, his size, relative lack of speed, and the same inability to get open that had plagued him his entire career rose up again, and his two years in Oakland were mostly forgettable.

He returned to the Packers in 1999, but the magic was gone. Ray Rhodes was the coach and the personnel were significantly different. He struggled to return kicks, got hurt again and was released at midseason, when he was picked up by Detroit.

Desmond Howard had his moment. It was one incredible season where everything fell into place for him and the Packers. Ironically, since Howard's first departure, the Packers have never been able to settle on a kick returner. So maybe the Packers needed Howard as much as Howard needed the Packers.

Strange Days Indeed

If you're looking for the darkest days in Green Bay Packers history, the days when it was truly trying just to be a Packers fan, look no further than 1986.

The Packers as an organization were floundering on the field and in the public consciousness. Forrest Gregg was going nowhere as head coach, the team was terrible, and the players were, well, not exactly living an exemplary lifestyle.

And the bottom was reached in 1986 when both star receiver James Lofton and cornerback Mossy Cade were charged in separate cases of sexual assault. In a surreal setting, both men went on trial in the same week and in the same Brown County courthouse (though in different courtrooms).

To add to the further weirdness of the situation, Gregg and his wife attended Cade's trial, sitting in the front row so the jury could see them, while Bart Starr and his wife were at Lofton's trial, again sitting in the front row in front of the jury.

"Imagine you're in the jury and you see Bart Starr sitting there," said one veteran Green Bay journalist who jumped from one courtroom to the other keeping track of the miscreant Packers. "It was a nutty week."

In the end Lofton was acquitted of his charges while Cade was convicted. But the damage had been done. In a searing *Sports Illustrated* expose, Green Bay was portrayed as a wayward NFL outpost where out-of-control players ran wild.

And even though Lofton was found not guilty, he was damaged goods, even in Green Bay. On draft day 1987, he was dealt to the Los Angeles Raiders for the paltry sum of a third- and a fourth-round pick.

Lofton has since been inducted into the Packers Hall of Fame and was a 2003 inductee into the Pro Football Hall of Fame.

Wayne's World

N o one ever could figure out linebacker Wayne Simmons. Blessed with as much natural ability as perhaps any player in the Ron Wolf-Mike Holmgren era, Simmons was a study in contradictions. He could play splendidly one game, as he did in the 1995 playoffs when the Packers upset the 49ers in San Francisco to mark this team's ascension to the big time. Or he could disappear for weeks on end, rarely making a play to the point where people wondered if he was even on the field.

He could be surly and unapproachable in the locker room and his glare at an approaching sports writer could be unforgettable. But while he could go weeks without talking, on those occasions when he did speak he was eloquent and thoughtful, and though no one knew it at the time, he ended up something of a tragic figure.

A first-round draft pick from Clemson in 1993, Simmons was part of the vanguard that would bring the Packers to NFL prominence. He had battled learning disabilities all his life, and several brushes with the law in college had turned some NFL teams away from him.

He settled into a role as the starting left outside linebacker but drew criticism for never being the kind of playmaker a first-round draft pick should be. But he was steady and disciplined and one of those players Holmgren could put out on the field and pretty much forget about because he knew the job would get done.

Never especially vocal either on the field or off, Simmons nonetheless had plenty so say to Holmgren the week before Super Bowl XXXI against the New England Patriots.

He had watched film all week of the Patriots' offense and, frankly, he wasn't impressed. He saw plenty of opportunities for the Packers' defense, which that season was ranked the best in the NFL, to accomplish a lot against young Patriots quarterback Drew Bledsoe. And while he voiced that to Holmgren, defensive coordinator Fritz Shurmur and his teammates, he was forbidden from telling the media.

"Just once?" Simmons pleaded.

"No," said Holmgren.

Holmgren had Super Bowl experience from his days as an assistant coach at San Francisco, and he knew the least little slip-up could be disastrous. He didn't want Simmons mouthing off about what the Packers' defense could do. It would just serve to infuriate the Patriots.

So Simmons sat and stewed and said nothing even though he was dying to tell everyone. As it turns out, of course, he was right. The Packers' defense played superbly, and the Packers rolled to the 35-21 victory, and it was only after the win that Simmons could say whet he felt.

That would be his last shining moment in Green Bay. After the season, he pursued free agency but didn't find the offers he was looking for. He came back to the Packers, but his job had already been taken by another free agent, Seth Joyner. In October, 1997 Simmons was traded to the Kansas City Chiefs for a fifth-round choice—not much compensation for a former first-rounder who had been a starter for four years.

Simmons retired after the 2001 season, and his life came to a premature and tragic end in the summer of 2002 when he died in a car crash in Kansas City.

The Ice Bowl

It remains the most memorable game in team history, and today there apparently isn't a single person who didn't attend it or didn't know of somebody who did.

It is the Ice Bowl, and it has taken on a life, a legend and a distinction of its own. In fact, no one really knows where the name "Ice Bowl" actually came from.

The specifics are now required learning in most elementary schools in Wisconsin and are as familiar to Packers fans as their phone numbers.

Lee Remmel, the Packers' veteran public relations director, is asked about the Ice Bowl more than any other game in team history, because it went so far in establishing the NFL as well as reinforcing just what Green Bay meant to the league.

But what many people forget is that this was the last hurrah for that Packers domination. When they beat the Dallas Cowboys on December 31, 1967 in 13-below weather and then went on to smack around the Oakland

Raiders in Super Bowl II, it signaled the end of one of greatest dynasties in pro sports.

Vince Lombardi quit as head coach to concentrate on general manager duties, and several key players retired. The following season, the Packers were 6-7-1 and wouldn't see the playoffs again until 1982 and wouldn't win another Super Bowl until 1997.

But for that time, for that moment, it was a special game that no one in Green Bay will likely ever forget. Indeed, fans today will still point to the spot in the end zone where Bart Starr sneaked in for the touchdown with 13 seconds remaining—a play only he knew was coming—for the win.

"I've answered more questions about that one play than probably everything that happened in my whole career," said Starr, who played 16 years for the Packers. "Even now, people ask me about that sneak in the Ice Bowl."

It wasn't so much that the game was especially well-played, though for the conditions, it was a remarkable performance. Indeed, that morning, as fans and players alike awoke to below-zero temperatures no one had expected the night before (a cold front came in faster than expected), there was some question whether the game would even be played.

But NFL commissioner Pete Rozelle, who was back on the West Coast for the AFL title game, was in constant contact with officials in Green Bay to monitor the weather. In the end, the decision was made at around 9 a.m. to go ahead and play. But it wasn't pretty.

With a stiff breeze that dropped the wind chill to 46 degrees below zero, players gave up any pretense of trying to stay warm. The heaters on the sidelines malfunctioned,

Conversations about the Green Bay Packers don't last five seconds without the name Vince Lombardi coming up. He was that important. *Photo courtesy of Vernon J. Biever*

the Packers band was told not to play because the brass instruments would freeze to their lips, and at least one player, Packers linebacker Ray Nitschke, suffered frostbite on his toes. Another player, Cowboys defense back Cornell Green, was believed initially to have suffered lung damage from breathing in the frigid air. But he was later given a clean bill of health.

And while the weather did keep some fans away, more than 40,000 people still showed up to watch a game fans who weren't even born then still talk about.

But when it was over and the Packers had survived a game that was already finding its place in league history, there was little celebrating in the Packers' locker room. The weather, the circumstances, the game had taken so much from this team that they just sat back against their lockers in total exhaustion. But there was something else.

"I think there was a dawning realization that they'd won a third straight [NFL] championship," Remmel said.

"It was a serious appreciation of what they'd accomplished."

And many probably also knew that those days—those wonderful, golden days—had come to an end.

Blood Money

Before there were any superstars in the fledgling NFL, there was Packers halfback Johnny McNally. In the late 1920s, McNally represented what the NFL was, what it wanted to be, and, in a very real sense, what it didn't want to be at the time. This was the so-called Iron Era of football, when tough guys played offense and defense and head protection consisted of a leather hat.

McNally was part of that era, a guy who loved to play the game so much that sometimes, he'd play even when he wasn't supposed to.

Back in the 1920s, the NFL was still looking for respectability. It was a sport decried by some as simple barbarism, a game which lacked the genteel quality of America's favorite game, baseball.

The league was also still dealing with scandals that found players hopping from one team to another and back again for extra pay. There was also the problem of college players showing up to play for pro teams to earn some quick cash.

McNally was no different. At St. John's College in Minnesota, he'd try to pick up some extra money playing in the new pro league, but he also knew that the league was cracking down. The answer to him seemed simple enough. He'd use an assumed name in the NFL. But what?

One day he was walking down the street with a buddy when they passed a movie theater that was playing the film *Blood and Sand* starring Rudolph Valentino.

That struck McNally immediately, and he told his friend, "You be Sand and I'll be Blood."

McNally played football for several years with the moniker Johnny Blood before joining the Packers and incorporating it all into Johnny "Blood" McNally.

Final Thoughts
From the Sidelines

Bob Harlan is right. The story of the Green Bay Packers is as much fiction as fact. But where does one start and the other begin?

Were there really players like Jim Taylor, Paul Hornung, Don Hutson, Tony Canadeo, Brett Favre, Jerry Kramer and Bart Starr, or do they only exist in our minds? Was the Packer Sweep the best play ever invented in the NFL and why did Reggie White really come to Green Bay when so many other teams wanted him to play with them? How does this franchise still survive when all the rules suggest it shouldn't? And what will we say 50 years from now when the Packers are part of some sociological study about football and its relationship to a city, to a state, to a country?

Maybe none of that really matters. Maybe it's just something to take at face value and enjoy.

But this much is clear. Many of the players who wore the Packers uniform over the years knew exactly what it meant to play there. Ray Nitschke, that tough linebacker who had to be dragged kicking and screaming off the field and toward retirement, never forgot.

And as the years went by, there was no bigger backer of the Packers than he was, and his surprising death from a heart attack in 1998 was mourned as though there had been a death in the family. And indeed, there had been.

Larry McCarren, the Pro Bowl center who stayed in Green Bay after retiring in 1984, and is now a local TV celebrity, knows too.

"I know it sounds corny," he said. "But everything I have today is a direct result of the Green Bay Packers. I came in as a 12th-round draft pick, and I was never a great player. But I became a good one, and I can thank the Green Bay Packers for that. It's a privilege to play this game, and it's a double privilege to play in Green Bay."

To adequately chronicle the Green Bay Packers would take more time and words than most of us could read. The stories are endless and the people unforgettable.

From Curly Lambeau to Mike Sherman and from Arnie Herber to Ahman Green, it's a story about men overcoming incredible odds in a place few would choose to come to on their own save for the fact that there's a great football story there.

Often a rookie free agent will be asked what he thinks about getting a chance to play for the Packers. And every time, the response is the same. Unbelievable. Unforgettable. Chance of a lifetime. Who wouldn't want to play for the Packers?

Many still can't believe this is a story that actually happened, and in today's world, it probably can't. But as NFL commissioner Paul Tagliabue said as he awarded the Packers the Lombardi Trophy for winning Super Bowl XXXI, this is probably the best thing that could have happened to the NFL.

And the story continues.

Celebrate the Heroes of Pro Football
in These Other Acclaimed Titles from Sports Publishing!

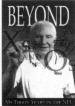

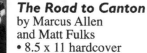
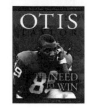